Bill Mahoney

a pilot's tale

the accidental wanderings of an aviator
through time and space

as written by himself

Dedicated in whole
to
life and living

and in part

to Lauren for opening some doors
and
to Guinevere for dreaming with me

Table of Contents

The FBO and Bill's Immortality

Bill Mahoney was meant to be a throw-away name, something that seemed to pop out of the deeper recesses of my mind without any conscious thought.[1] Little did I realize that it would live on and on in the aviation community for decades until it became a sort of mythic cult phrase; an inside joke similar to Ayn Rand's question of "who is John Galt?" or the Fight Club's mantra of "His Name is Robert Paulson."

It was a name created in the heat of the moment in response to a question I had not thought to ask.

Decades later I returned to the scene of the crime, the headwaters and nexus of my misadventures. For reasons that will become clear, it was still judicious for me to use a pseudonym and maintain some sort of vast distance between who I was and what I had done in an earlier life.

"Does Dale still run line service?" I asked the evening line crew as they lounged about the FBO[2], waiting for the occasional airplane to taxi in, request fuel, make a pit stop and continue its cross-county journey.

It had been 25 years, and yet the layout was much the same. Low-paid workers on the evening shift hanging about, telling lies to each other and waiting for closing time. Afterwards, a trip to the bar and more lies. Maybe pick up a girl if all the stars aligned.

---

[1]   I have often believed these messages are sent from our higher selves, free of the filters which often mask our speech and cloud our deeper thoughts. Some refer to these as 'Freudian Slips.'

[2]   Fixed Base Operator. A sort of 7-11 / Jiffy Lube / Maintenance Shop / Passenger Terminal for small-and-medium sized non-commercial airplanes. Everything from Cessna 150s to Lear Jets to Gulfstreams might stop here on a given day. When not flying, pilots may spend a good part of their lives hanging out in FBOs, waiting to receive customers or other marching orders. In the 1980s many of the pilot lounges were little more than mosh pits with vending machines and stale coffee. Today, the tonier FBOs offer extreme boutique services and treat pilots as the gods some imagine themselves to be.

"Yeah, he still runs the place, but he is out for some minor surgery," said the desk jockey. "He'll be back in a couple of weeks if you want to stop by again."

"No," I said. "I used to work for him a long time ago. Doing what you guys do, also on the night shift. I just happened to be passing through and wanted to say hello."

"Sure," came the reply. "Can we get a name and tell him who stopped by?"

It was a moment of truth. So, I gave them my name.

"Tell him Bill Mahoney stopped by to say hello."

"What?????" came his reply, and four sets of eyes locked onto me.

"Bill Mahoney," I said evenly.

"You are not Bill Mahoney," he responded while making a circular motion with his hand, indicating not just the room but the whole universe. "We are all Bill Mahoney."

"No, you are not," I said reflexively. "I am Bill Mahoney."

"Bullshit mister," said another voice from across the room as laughter began to creep through the discussion. "We are all Bill Mahoney."

"NO, you are not," I declared as I swung around the room, looking each impostor in the eye. And to emphasize my point I spoke slowly:

I
AM
BILL
MAHONEY

THE
BILL
MAHONEY

"You can't be," said the leader. "Come on, who are you really? Who can we tell Dale came to call?"

I was stunned, nearly speechless and wildly amused. Decades after I had invented him, Bill Mahoney had not died. He was apparently alive, well and healthy. He might be ordering pizza tonight or trying to pick up a chick at the local bar. He might still be buying fuel. He might be calling for a delivery at the lumberyard. Hell, he may even have gotten himself into some tight and uncomfortable spots. A guy can make a lot of mischief in a quarter of a century.

It was a Ray Ban moment, and I placed the Aviators over my eyes despite the darkening skies.

"When Dale comes back," I finished evenly, "tell him Bill Mahoney dropped in to say hello. THE Bill Mahoney. The original. The One. He will know exactly who you were talking to."

And with that I walked out the door as my namesakes, now multi-generational in depth, starred at my back in disbelief.

I had achieved, accidentally, what all great men of history secretly long for.

I am Bill Mahoney.

I am immortal.

Get a name . . .

"We can't keep selling av gas to customers without a name," said Rona, a petite bombshell with platinum hair and an aura that seemed to say she was going to have a good time (and meant it). To a twenty-year-old male she was a sort of enigma – a 50-year-old woman who had clearly not given up her pursuit of the opposite sex. She was my mother's age but clearly not of my mother's disposition. Did people her age have sex?

As the face of customer service at the airport FBO, she was a favorite with all the transient pilots who made their way earthward in search of fuel. At that time, it was a given article of faith that front-line desk personnel would be chatty, smoking hot and cater to the egos of the male pilot world. One regional FBO even gave away raw steaks with a certain amount of fuel purchased and was rumored to offer complete 'full-service' if a pilot had a few hours to kill.

But when the sun went down so did the traffic. Because incoming aircraft were few and far between, the evening vibe at most FBOs was considerably more relaxed. It tended to promote loafing and a sort of languishing about; more reminiscent of small-town barber shops than hustle-and-bustle airports.

We might go hours without a customer and then get a sudden influx, the airport Unicom announcing that a wayward aviator was headed our way. Sometimes the sale involved local pilots who needed 10 gallons. On other occasions cross-county business jets would taxi in, arriving with their minimum fuel requirements and purchasing 800 gallons of JetA.

"Well hell Rona, these are cash sales," I replied. "We've got their N number.[3] What more do we need?"

"Doesn't matter," she shot back. "Accounting is on my butt. Get a name."

---

[3]   N numbers are unique identifiers the Federal Aviation Administration assigns to a civilian aircraft. Each country has their own prefix (N for United States, C for Canada, G for Great Britain, D for Germany, etc...) followed by a limited combination of numbers and/or letters. Some owners like Donald Trump will encode their initials into the registration in a sort of ultimate vanity plate (N725DT) while other owners wish for anonymity.

This was slightly problematic in 1980. The world had not yet embraced ATMs, Apple Pay, credit cards or signs that proclaimed plastic as the only acceptable means of payment. Many legitimate pilots (and some who weren't) were flying around the country and paying with big wads of cash coming out of their pockets.

And names were problematic for another sort of reason. Although not technically illegal, our night crew had been selling super-high octane av gas (aviation grade airplane fuel) to the automotive racing crowd.

It started innocently enough with some guy wandering in one night with a five gallon can asking if he could buy some 115/145 for his drag car and pay cash. We consented, made up an N number to satisfy the sales ticket and put 'Cash' as the name.

Soon enough his buddies were showing up, asking for 20 gallons here and 20 gallons there. That business, coupled with a steady stream of aviators paying with Uncle Sam's Federal Reserve Notes were putting our accounting department in a tailspin.

"I don't make the rules," said Rona with her best death stare. "You got to have a name associated with each sale."

When the evening shift arrived, I announced the new accounting requirement. Each sale required a name.

One of the more intelligent loafers reminded me that – as the person behind the desk – it would be my job to confront customers and demand a name.

"Okay," I replied, "from here on out every cash sale will be to Bill Mahoney."

But who was Bill Mahoney, and why did he percolate out of my subconsciousness?

It was an easy reach.

Before this job I had worked at a small daily newspaper in the Midwest. This paper was part of a media chain that was eventually sold multiple times before morphing into its current, and much diminished, state.

Although paying phenomenally low wages, this newspaper managed to attract an ensemble cast of top-notch reporters and photographers.[4] It is still a mystery how this wide spot in the road managed to draw in such talent. But that was the thing back in the 1980s. Journalism was an honest profession and everyone coming out of J-school had to start at the bottom and pay their dues.

Really good talent rose up-and-out of the local ranks quickly; those of a more modest talent or without soaring ambitions could work their whole career in one place and make a sustainable, if not opulent, living.

---

[4] I was hired as a part-time photographer and my boss – who showed up from god-knows-where without a degree – won national awards during his tenure. He beat out talent from Los Angeles and New York City and San Jose and Topeka. He had an incredible eye for detail that I often missed.

Some mornings we would drive around town, looking for a front-page shot while racing against a hard deadline of 11 a.m. More often than not, I was nursing a hangover from the night before while he lived a life of strict abstinence. We would grab a couple of shots, race back to the photo lab and develop our negatives. When dried, we would lay the 36-exposure roll on top of a light table and use an 8X magnifying loupe to select a single image.

The negative was then inserted into our Leica enlarger and projected onto a sheet of Kodak's quick-drying Polycontrast photo paper. It would spend 90 seconds in the developer, 30 seconds in the stop bath, and 5 minutes in the fixer.

What would emerge from this wondrous red-light world would be a beautiful image, my boss capturing a moment in time that I – standing two feet away and by his side – never even saw. And although I would later become a photojournalism instructor at a respected Midwest Journalism school, I would never approach the level of 'seeing' that my boss possessed. You either have the eye or you don't.

This specific newspaper was a thriving and profitable enterprise with approximately 25 full-time employees. The stars, at least in my opinion, were the writers[5] who carried their ever-present notepads with them and scribbled indecipherable notes in the margins.

Every morning, they would come dragging in, look over their notes, stare at the clock and begin pounding out stories on state-of-the-art IBM Selectric typewriters.

You could always tell the bad typists by a certain staccato machine gun sound, signifying an untold number of XX's striking the paper and crossing out the last sentence.

When satisfied with their triple-spaced output, the raw copy moved on to the editor's desk. The editor would rework the story, making great red marks here and there and scribbling secret code on the side for the next-in-line typesetters.

The typesetters would transcribe the work into special computers, spitting out the story on two-inch wide paper. There were no errors allowed in this typesetting, no auto correct feature and no going back.

What keys the typesetters touched became the gospel for the day. And all under the pressure of the ever-looming daily deadline, with clocks lining every wall to remind us that eternity was ticking down.

The typesetter output would then be handed over to the layout crew, who waxed the backside using a special machine. This group began the precise and tedious work of laying out the headlines and stories in their own aesthetic.

---

[5] There was always a historical (and philosophical) split between the editorial side of the house and the advertisement side. The News/Editorial group saw themselves as pure and noble, driven by a desire to always tell the truth. They saw the ad side of the house as a bunch of whores selling their soul to the devil. It seldom occurred to the News/Editorial set that their vaunted purity was bought and paid for on the backs of the ad men.

The look and feel of the newspaper was created here, page by page. Annual contests would honor the best and brightest of these efforts, hand-crafted and touched by the human mind, deciding how a story or ad or photograph would be displayed.

From there, each individual page was sent to the back shop, where full sized negatives were created, placed in vacuum carriers sandwiched against tin plates, and exposed to tremendously intense carbon arc light.

This blinding light was like the sun creating a new world, and the reverse image from the negative became eternally etched on the plate, much like those flash-fried ghost shadows from Hiroshima.

The plates were separated from the negatives, and a chemical wash applied to bring out the raised impressions made by the artificial sun. As a last step, the plates were dried and taken to the press room.

In the press room, technicians would begin the precise work of installing each plate, adjusting the ink baths of the offset rollers and aligning the multi-ton paper feeds into the gigantic press machine.

At 2 p.m. (it was always 2 p.m. for that was the deadline) the principal pressman would hit a red button, causing a loud klaxon to sound and bringing the beast to life.

It was my favorite time of day, and I endeavored whenever I could to be present for the birthing process.

Fa-TISH, Fa-TISH, Fa-TISH the beast would say in a painfully slow cadence as if awakening from a deep slumber. The floors would shake, and the walls would echo as the press came to life, slowly picking up speed like one of those old steam locomotives leaving the station.

As the seconds rolled on the beast would begin to come into its own, finding its rhythm and speed. All the while technicians were running around, twisting knobs and dials to adjust the rollers; toning down the ink; adjusting the folding mechanisms and attending to a thousand details as they scanned the output for the perfect blend of pressure between plates, the offset mat and the newsprint that was running without end through it all.

In a matter of minutes, the press would be running at full speed. The beast was ingesting massive amounts of paper from the endless rolls, threading just-inked newsprint through a bewildering series of up-and-down motions. At the far end, some mechanical magic was bringing all this chaos together; cutting, sorting, folding and spitting out the product known as a newspaper.

As if to put an exclamation point on the process, there was a unique and unforgettable smell associated with the press. Perhaps it was a mixture of ink, hydraulic fluids, electric motors, heated rubber mats and metal-on-metal friction whose scent remains deep in my memory.

I would try to take it all in and stand in awe as the beast cranked out an average of 3,200 copies every day, six days a week. If there is such a thing as modern alchemy, I would nominate the old pressmen as its wizards.

I always left that space feeling better about the world; that we had somehow managed to win the fight and bring a modicum of enlightenment to our readers, that we were participating in a small but perceptible lifting of the veil.

Nikola Tesla once said that if we wished to understand the universe we needed to think in terms of energy, frequency and vibration. To that I would add smell.

Our star reporter was a recent J-school graduate from the University of Kansas. He was east coast raised, sharp as a tack and his beat covered city and county government. The articles he wrote cast a harsher light than perhaps many would have preferred.

He was not uncovering malfeasance or corruption as much as giving the officials a platform to show off their own incompetence or lack of understanding. They took advantage of these opportunities on a startlingly regular basis.

As such, many people who could recognize his byline ('story by James Brown') would not have been able to identify him in a police lineup. But it is also true that in every Midwest town of 10,000 people, the locals can spot and smell a stranger from a thousand miles away.

So, when James went out to drink[6], he found it prudent to identify himself not as James Brown the reporter/agitator, but rather as Clarence Mahoney.

This proved to be a safer bet but confused the locals who could not recall any member of any Mahoney clan ever settling down in Kansas.

If Clarence Mahoney was good enough for James, then I figured he must have a younger brother named Bill.

Thus, Bill Mahoney came into existence, fully imagined to satisfy some unknown person in the accounting department and hopefully making their life a bit less harried.

Much like those vaunted illegal aliens who are given bogus social security numbers and are faithfully paying taxes into a system in which they will never be able to collect, Mr. Mahoney's name began popping up all over town; ordering pizza, getting cabs and appearing in innumerable ledgers when the opposing party asked for a name.

---

[6] In the 1980s this town – like most in the Midwest - had a virtual cornucopia of bars and clientele. There was the rock-n-roll bar with local and regional talent showing up on occasion. There was the obligatory cowboy bar. There was a speak easy in a downtown basement. There was a gun-and-knife bar where you were either welcome or not.

There was a decrepit pool hall where old-timers played dominoes and cast a wary eye on anyone younger than 60. There was a version of New York's Flatiron building up against the tracks where the down-and-out seemed to congregate.

And of course, there was an exclusive country club, accessible only through private membership or connected friends. All those old watering holes are gone now, and the post-pandemic world (along with a few suspicious fires) have emptied the town of a rich and divergent watering hole culture.

Lumber yard pickup? Hold for Bill Mahoney. Name given at the front door of a private club? Bill Mahoney. Attempt to pick up girls at the bar? Bill Mahoney.

He also began to buy an ever-increasing amount of av gas[7]. His cash purchases came to be associated with a specific N number. None of it was – strictly speaking – true. Yet none of his purchases were patently false.

In short, everyone began to use the name Bill Mahoney. The throw-away name got legs, ran down the street, out of town, clean out of the state and somehow - into immortality.

---

[7]   115/145 av gas is seriously potent fuel. It was formulated during WWII to help aircraft engines extract the maximum amount of power out of a given gallon as gasoline. It burns hotter and more completely than any other type of gasoline on the market (and contains the dreaded additive of lead).

Thinking that my decrepit car could use some additional horsepower, I unadvisedly dumped 5 gallons into the tank one night. The car ran like the devil himself but would not shut off once fuel got into the cylinders. Ignition off? Doesn't matter. Car still running. Try to flood the engine? Doesn't matter. Car still running. Gun the engine with the key off? Doesn't matter. Car still running.

I am in the parking lot of the FBO with a car that smells like it is burning av gas, knocking and pinging loud enough to raise eyebrows (and nostrils). Solution? Drive to the gas station and try to dilute the devil's brew with the lowest grade fuel I can find. Drive around like fury for an hour or so, pray to god the cylinders will cool down enough to stop the endless pre-ignition damage, and resolve to never again put pilfered, high-octane fuel in a low-compression engine.

Beginnings

When I was six years old, I had a dream. I think it was more than a dream for the images and sensations it suggests still reverberate in my head and speak to my soul all these many years later.

In my dream I was walking through a small, plowed garden just across the street from Aunt Lillian & Uncle Wilbur's house. I began to run and instantly flew upward. I knew I was headed to heaven. As I got closer, I could hear music. It was emanating from two pillars, each made of music but suggesting some sort of form. As I passed between the pillars the world went bright, filled with light and bliss. I wish I could say I saw God, but that would be false to the story. The world just went to bliss.

Growing up in a small Midwest town was a series of contrasts and contradictions. On one hand, small-town America in the 1960s offered a safe haven to fully explore the world. A Schwinn bicycle, sixty-three cents for lunch and a trusting mother meant you could stay out all day and come home when the sun went down.

In those heady days, a sort of pro-creationist nirvana arrived with a full head of steam. World War II aviators, having painted their bombers with images of naked women, returned in a fever dream.

They were eager to forget the war, host card parties and procreate as if they were all Catholic. Every family in our neighborhood had at least two children (we had four) and longed for a color TV and a roof-mounted antenna.

On the other hand, small town America was also terribly parochial and close-looped. Without cable TV, we were limited to pointing our fragile antennas to the southeast, hoping to pick up the only three network channels available, and interpreting images and voice through the ever-present white snow that cursed long-distance viewing.

As an article of faith, Walter Cronkite would show up every night and tell us the news. It was a time of innocence and naivety, for we believed him when he spoke. After the sun went down and the ionosphere began to cool, we could catch the far away FM radio stations of Kansas City and listen to the latest rock-and-roll.[8]

As a child, my brother and I had free range during the summer to take us as far as our legs would carry. In practice, that meant the city limits of our 6 square mile world.

The town had a series of concrete-lined drainage ditches, and we would spend endless hours traipsing through the open portals and occasionally daring to enter dark passages as they passed underneath the streetscape.

Once I was wading in the ditch after a torrential downpour. The water swept my legs out from under me, and I headed swiftly towards a dark tunnel full of jagged pipes and rocks. A hand caught me by the scruff of the neck and hauled me to dry ground. It was Tim, someone's older brother. I think he saved my life. He has no memory of the event.

During one birthday my twin and I received Schwinn bicycles from an authorized dealer operating out of his garage. These transportation devices increased our range significantly and allowed us to peddle our way westward towards the country club and its exclusive[9] (but tiny) swimming pool.

---

[8]   Although Kansas City was considered a medium-sized radio market, there was still a limited selection of who and what received airplay. Decades later I would come to realize that a great river of other musicians — whom I never heard while growing up in the Midwest — had left a deep groove in the psyche of both coasts while passing over the Plains in relative obscurity.

[9]   Even in small towns there can exist a pecking order, a sort of perceived hierarchy. If your family was hip, you belonged to 'the club.' If not, you swam at the gigantic city swimming pool, played golf at the municipal course and took advantage of their public tennis courts.

On the west edge of town was the municipal airport with its 3,500-foot-long main runway and a crosswind grass strip. It sat at 1001 feet above sea level, hosted an FAA Flight Service Station and was home to a large hangar full of airplanes. This was a time when an average man, pulling down an average salary, supporting an average family and living in an average house, could afford to fly. And if he were above average, he could own his own airplane.

Every time I peddled by the airport I would stop and watch the traffic come and go. One day an Army Huey helicopter landed, and as the crew walked toward the diner, I jumped the fence and made myself at home in one of the rear sling seats. I must have been lost in my own world because I never saw the pilot approach and ask what I was doing in his machine.

This aviator looked me over, broke a dozen Army regulations and asked if I wanted a ride. I said "yes," and we were soon hovering above the ground, making that wop-wop-wop[10] sound so peculiar to the Huey while its insides shook in syncopated harmony. The short ride was over in a matter of minutes, but the thrill remained, and I began to dream of flying.

One time I was at the airport and a small experimental aircraft came in for a landing. It was a single-seat Bowers Fly Baby painted in pre-WWII colors of blue and yellow. It sailed over the fence and made a perfect landing before taxiing to the ramp.

I watched the pilot carefully maneuver around the fuel pump, swing the tail around sharply and kill the engine in one fluid motion. As he took off his leather helmet a cascade of long, flowing auburn hair fell around her shoulders and came to rest on her leather jacket. She ran her fingers quickly through her mane and shook it like a lion. A woman, an aviator, a goddess. An image that would remain, even years later as I flew my own Bowers around the countryside.

---

10   My father owned a tire store and like everyone during that time, displayed a surprising range of politically incorrect signage. One such sign showed a wagon wheel with boots attached to every spoke. The sign read: "New Italian mud and snow tire. Dago thru mud, Dago thru snow, and when Dago flat, Dago wop-wop-wop."

As I entered my teenage years, a local pilot / business entrepreneur named Fred took me under his wings and sort of adopted[11] me. He would take me flying, and on Sundays a large contingent of local aviators would gather and fly 50 miles west into a small town for a hamburger and coke.

This town, which should have been more correctly described as a tiny hamlet, had been a water stop for steam locomotives in the late 1800s, then later a regional hot spot for cowboys and finally a destination for area aviators.

It had a small grass strip running north/south and you taxied onto the main street while looking for a place to park. Good aviators could land a twin-engine airplane on the tiny strip, but it was getting out that presented a larger problem. When the summer heat hit and the air became thin, it was everything some of the smaller planes could do to lift off: applying full power as the grass strip ran downhill to the south, counting on the engine not to fail and hoping their performance calculations were accurate.

When I was in 9th grade, I joined the football team at the strong urging of my father. He was a great sportsman and, despite his smaller stature, excelled at everything he touched. Me, not so much.

The coach posted his roster on the locker room wall. By my name he wrote "center." I soon learned what that entailed.

First down, hike the ball and get hit. Second down, hike the ball and get hit. Third down, hike the ball and get hit. Fourth down and short yardage, hike the ball and get hit by multiple linemen.

---

[11] It was years before I came to understand that my adoption was a kind of healing for Fred, whose infant son was run over before his eyes by a passing tractor-trailer. Had he lived, his son would have been my age.

I traded that position for a camera, preferring to document the brutality as opposed to participating in it. Photography became both a passion and a career of sorts for many years to come.

During my junior year, the guidance counselors were poking and probing, asking us what we wanted to be in life when we grew up. I had some different ideas than they were proposing, perhaps to my detriment.

I informed them I wanted to fall out of airplanes.

Life At The Drop Zone

At age 16, I began a relentless campaign against my parents, seeking their permission to make a skydive. My oldest brother – who in many respects remains my soulish twin – had been skydiving and flying for years. It seemed like I wanted to follow in his footsteps.

The age of consent to skydive is 18, so it took months for me to obtain their signature and make my first jump in the middle of Kansas. On the way to my weekend lesson, I picked up a couple of hitchhikers. They were from the area and had knowledge of the skydiving center.

"Some chick died there last week," the traveler casually volunteered. "Her chute didn't open."

As I let them off and headed down the nondescript road toward the skydiving center, the ramifications gave me great pause. Was this really a smart idea?

The center itself was nestled in the middle of a huge but abandoned WWII naval air base. The physical reminders of neglect and decay were everywhere as I made my way around the perimeter roads.

But now and again I noticed signs of industrial life. A school bus company, tucked away around a corner. A fiberglass manufacturer down the road. A Junior College agricultural substation off on another road. And strangest of all, the state's one and only official law enforcement training center.

As I pulled into the skydiving center's parking lot, I watched a figure ride in against the sun. He was of large stature, challenging the tiny Honda CT-70's meager output. He parked next to me and shut off the engine. He looked upward, listening intently for something I could not perceive.

Suddenly, and with a surprising fluidity of motion, he pulled a rifle out from the motorcycle's curiously mounted gun rack, aimed upward and fired a single shot. A pigeon fell out of the sky and landed with a thud beside my feet. He placed his rifle back in the gun rack, kick-started the tiny Honda and drove off without a word.

I headed inside, found a skydiver packing a chute and asked him the foremost question on my mind.

"Did some girl die here last week skydiving?" I asked with trepidation.

"No," came the immediate reply and my countenance lifted.

Then as an afterthought he said, "it was two weeks ago."

"Who was that janitor and what's his deal?" I asked in a new line of questioning.

"You mean the guy on the Honda?" He's not the janitor.[12] He owns the place."

"He owns the skydiving center?" I asked for clarification.

"No," said the jumper as he continued to inspect his chute across the long and narrow table. "That is Sal. He owns the base. We just rent from him."

"What about the Junior College and the bus company and the training academy?" I asked, still reeling from my cognitive dissonance.

"Yeah, they rent from him as well. He is everybody's landlord."

---

[12] Many years later I worked in the Marketing department of a business jet company. I had just moved up the ranks from technical writer to contract administrator and was tasked with bringing paperwork upstairs to a client meeting. As I stepped into the room, I saw my coworker in a suit with a poorly-dressed young man sitting across the table from him. I assumed he was the janitor.

I dropped off the paperwork and later asked my coworker who the loser was and what he was doing in the office. "Oh, he's the lead singer of group xyz and they just bought an $8,000,000 airplane. He was here to spec it out."

The philosopher Anais Nin once observed that 'We don't see the world as it is, we see the world as we are.' Apparently, I have always seen myself as a janitor.

"Where does he live?" I asked, thinking about the vast and decaying landscape.

The jumper pointed out the west-facing window. "In the control tower."

"How could a fellow who looks like a bum afford to own a whole airbase" I wondered aloud.

"His mom bought it for him," came the reply. "She was tired of him getting underfoot and figured he couldn't cause too much trouble out here in the middle of nowhere."

"Did it work?" I inquired cautiously, feeling like a guy who had already asked one too many personal questions of a stranger.

"Not so much," he said with a laugh.

I introduced myself and told him I was scheduled for their first jump training class. He informed me that I was their only student. Something about a schedule mix up.

"Do I need to come back another weekend?" I asked while contemplating a three-hour car ride back home.

"No, it's fine," he said. "I guess they told you we have space if you want to sleep here for the weekend."

"Yes, and I brought my sleeping bag."

"Pick a spot down the hall, there's plenty of room."

Indeed, there was. The skydiving center was located in an old barracks. Built in a 'H' configuration and two stories tall, it once housed 300 men. Now you could skateboard or ride a bicycle inside the endless and mostly gutted arms of the structure.

Although much of the plumbing and electricity had been ripped out when the base was deactivated, the military left or forgot several old metal bunk beds. I made my way down the hall and noted that many of the beds appeared to be occupied. I found an empty spot and made myself at home.

The place had a definite hippie commune sort of vibe, and I came to understand that an ever-rotating number of chronically under-employed skydivers[13] were calling the place home.

After stashing my backpack under one of the less filthy bunks, I made my way outside just in time to hear a rustle overhead. It was the sound of parachutes opening, and experienced jumpers were coming in for a landing in the center's front yard.

I watched as the group maneuvered their rectangular parachutes in tight spirals toward the small yard. One of the jumpers was slightly off course and appeared to be headed for the power lines. He flew right into them, pulled down hard on his steering toggles and dropped straight down between the tangle of lines.

At two feet off the ground, he cut-away (disconnected) his parachute from his harness, rolled forward in a somersault and landed on his feet. He looked up at his parachute now suspended in the overhead lines.

Having no earthly idea if this was a normal landing, I asked a skydiver who was standing nearby and watching it all.

"Are you kidding?" he said gazing at the scene. "That was a no shit miracle you just witnessed."

As we looked, the 155,000-volt main line began to snap and crackle. Suddenly there was a gigantic explosion. The power line melted the parachute, sent a bolt of lightning down through the now liquid nylon lines and blew an impressive hole in the ground. The entire south end of the base lost power.

About 15 minutes later an electrical crew came by to make things right. They removed the goo from the power lines and looked at the charred ground.

"Did you know him?" they asked a jumper who was still staring up at the mess.

"Pretty well" he said. "It was me."

---

13   Typically known as 'jump bums' in the skydiving vernacular.

My training for the first jump lasted about four hours and I had this Zen notion in my mind. Train on Saturday, contemplate life Saturday night and jump sometime Sunday.

I had been practicing cutaways in the back room, fitted with an old parachute harness and hoisted heavenward by a boat trailer ratchet. The instructor would crank me a few feet off the ground, give me a gentle spin and command me to 'cutaway' or release the main parachute from its harness. Like most of the training equipment from that time, the center used surplus military gear. I would be jumping what the industry called a 'cheapo'. Very comforting.

Suspended thus, I would practice releasing the canopy system, fall a few feet onto an obviously surplus military mattress and try to execute a PLF (Parachute Landing Fall). The instructor hoisted me up again, gave me a spin and looked down the hall.

"He's ready," he said shouting into the distance.

"He, who?" I said to no one in particular. I still had in my mind an entire evening to contemplate life, the universe and mortality.

"All right," said the instructor as he watched one last cutaway. "Let's get you suited up."

Sufficiently freaked out, I followed him to the front room. They handed me a jumpsuit that made me look more like a filling station attendant and less like the skygod I had envisioned. Everybody has their first jump story and mine was not unique.

Scared, anxious and with an abnormal amount of adrenaline, we waddled to the Cessna 185 and climbed in. On the way to altitude (2,800 feet for me) the experienced jumpers began to quietly taunt me. Because I would be first out and jump using a static line, I was facing forward toward the instrument panel. The experienced jumpers sat in the back and after dropping me off, would ride up to 9,500 feet for their freefall.

Behind me I could feel one of the jumpers poking and prodding my main chute container, inspecting it. In a voice loud enough for me to overhear but supposedly whispered to his fellow co-conspirator, he wondered if the chute would open. Given the fatality from a few weeks earlier, it made me extremely nervous.

21

As we banked left and lined up on jump run, the jumpmaster ensured my static line was hooked up and swung open the hinged door. A profound sensory input of turbulent air and burnt av gas flooded into the cockpit as the pilot slowed the plane to 80 mph.

On command I climbed out onto the strut and faced forward. The jumpmaster slapped me on the thigh and said "GO!"

Over the wind noise I looked back at him and - incredulous as it sounds - said, "ME???"

"GO" he shouted again.

"NOW"? I asked as if someone was going to call my bluff and tell me this was all just a big joke.

"NOW!" he shouted and struck me forcefully on the thigh. I released my hand hold on the strut, spread out as they had instructed and quickly felt the pull of the parachute as it began extracting itself from the container.

In seconds I was under canopy - under a cheapo - and floating down towards earth. It was a short three-minute ride. The landing zone was in a plowed field halfway down the runway and I landed without incident. What a rush! The center's ancient Chevy pickup collected me, and we headed back to the barracks.

In the evening, the skydiving bums living at the center convinced me that I owed them a case of beer for my first jump. I would come to discover that skydivers had many rules and rituals in which someone always seemed to owe someone else a case of beer.

I was 16 and experiencing what few people do at that age. I was highly impressionable and about to become immersed into the EFS[14] world.

---

[14]   Eat, Fuck, Skydive. My brother gave me a stylish hoodie that I proudly wore to church for many a year until I realized the cloud structure said in squiggly line art: Eat, Fuck, Skydive. Really? Thankfully none of my fellow brethren seemed to notice the non-theological message on my chest.

A World Unto Itself . . .

It's very difficult to convey the full spectrum impact skydiving held for me. After that first jump, I began spending most weekends at the skydiving center, commonly referred to as the DZ (Drop Zone).

It was beautiful, cosmic, wacky, zany, crazy, enlightening and surreal all at the same time. It was tremendous fun. It involved an element of risk that inevitably attracted a certain type of personality. It expanded my consciousness in a very real way. It taught me to live in the moment. It was everything a young man could ask for.

People have been jumping out of airplanes since the early days of aviation, but usually because the wings fell off or some other catastrophic emergency had occurred. Pilots who were forced to jump received automatic but unofficial membership in the 'Caterpillar Club.' While a few barnstormers incorporated parachuting acts during the 1920s, it was not until the late 1950s that people began to consider jumping out of airplanes as a recreational activity.

Early pioneers in the sport had no instruction manuals to guide them. They jumped surplus military gear, and it was a revelation when they began to understand that a body in freefall could be controlled. With this knowledge, they could leave the aircraft at the same time, fly their bodies together and create 4-man formations before separating and opening their parachutes.

This flying together was known as RW (relative work) and became the basis for most skydiving activities through today. Jumping out of bigger airplanes allowed for larger formations, and when I entered the sport military rigs had given way to custom-made sport parachutes and 30-man formations.

Learning to skydive happened in progressive steps. At first you were attached to a static line and given a dummy ripcord. If you could locate and pull the dummy ripcord three times in a row, they would take you up a little higher and let you actually deploy your parachute. This was an early milestone for both student and instructor and known in the business as a *hop-and-pop*.

These three-step progressions continued at higher and higher altitudes; now successfully waiting 5 seconds before pulling the ripcord, then 10 second delays, 15 second delays, 20 second delays and finally 30 second delays. All the time falling by yourself while the jumpmaster watched a receding speck[15] head towards earth.

This slow progression was also designed to help students begin to maneuver their body through space. A left turn was accomplished by tucking the left shoulder down and kicking out the right leg slightly. A mid-air flip was accomplished by bringing the arms in sharply, letting the head go vertical and stopping the somersault with legs compressed then outstretched. It was ballet and flying, and although the wind was ferocious there was no sense of falling. It was more like being supported on a column of air, free of time and space.

At the conclusion of all this preliminary training, you were invited into the world of RW.

As the newbie, your position was always 'base.' This meant you left the airplane first and allowed the other jumpers to fly to you, linking up hands as they flew their bodies to yours. You learned not to reach out, for this changed the air and would cause the formation to break up. If you came flying down to the group and did not stop your forward momentum in time, this would likewise collapse the formation. That was known as 'funneling the formation' and would most likely cost you the sport's standard penalty - a case of beer.

When I started jumping there was an old hippie/gypsy vibe that ran throughout the sport. Because it was so new and small in numbers, all the founding members knew one another and occupied a sort of gods-of-mount-Olympus stature. They were nomads traversing the land in vans and old school buses, living only to jump. They would show up from Arizona or California and spend a week at our DZ, teaching us by example how to fly.

This gypsy lifestyle was cross cultural and communal. If you showed up at a new drop zone with just the gear on your back, you would inevitably be invited into someone's home for a day or a week. It was a community in the very best sense of the word, and while others were running around India

---

15   It was startling to see how quickly a jumper disappeared from view once they left the airplane. Within 12 seconds they were falling at 120 miles per hour and had dropped 2,000 feet below the airplane. Jumpmasters couldn't really see much of their student at this point.

seeking inner peace, we were living it at the drop zones throughout the States.

The sport attracted a super diverse group of people, from strait-laced military personnel to seriously wild and crazy freaks. These divergent personality types would have never connected in a normal life, but in the air - in pursuit of this dream - we were all brothers.

Sometimes in freefall, time would get altered and maneuvers would seem to happen in super slow motion. Athletes call this state 'being in the zone.' My friends used to ask what it felt like to freefall and I would tell them 'It feels like being god.'

It was an incomplete answer trapped by language. As I developed a deeper spiritual sense in later years, I think what I was trying to say was that it brought me fully into the present moment in which I felt a deep connection with the divine.

These experiences carved deep and lasting neural pathways in my brain. I remember some of them like it was yesterday.

_____

One day while in freefall, three of us had linked together at around 6,000 feet. Richard, the fourth member of our team, was built stout and solid, and had eyeglasses like coke bottles. The trio watched as Richard swooped down and came flying at us like a freight train. He was hauling ass and ready to take out the formation.

We quickly unlinked as he sped through. Regrouping, we watched as he pivoted in midair and made a second run at us. Upon closer inspection I could see that he was winking at us, one eye open, one eye closed in a repeating pattern. Again, he came at us like a freight train and the formation separated to let him pass through the open space.

Looking at each other and using hand signals, we called off any further attempt to link up.

On the ground, Richard told us that one of his eyeglass lens had blown out and that he was having trouble judging distance, looking at us from one eye and then another. No shit Richard.

On another jump we had completed our formation and separated from each other before opening at 2,500 feet. From that altitude it's about a 3-minute ride under canopy. I was floating down, enjoying the panorama and looking for a suitable place to land.

The sun began to blink on and off and a whistling sound came from that general direction. Within seconds the whistle had become a roar and Sal, the air base owner, buzzed us in his sailplane. Because they have no engine, sailplanes are virtually silent at low air speed. As they pick up speed, the wind noise over the airframe increases exponentially.

We watched as Sal screamed by us at 160 miles an hour, lifted the nose into the air and executed a perfect barrel roll. He pushed the nose over and built-up speed before buzzing us again. In today's world it might be considered stupid, but at the time it was thrilling and great fun.

———————

Another skydiver was also a pilot and owned an aerobatic Pitts. He liked to fly fast and upside down, hence became known as Fast Eddie. One day he taxied up in his little biplane. The top of his rudder was green, and we could not figure out what had caused the discoloration.

"Well," he offered. "I was doing a little inverted flying over the wheat field. I may have gotten a little closer to the ground than I realized."

———————

With about 45 jumps under my belt, I had to use my reserve parachute. We had been doing some '4-way RW' and had separated for opening. I had recently replaced my D-ring ripcord handle with a much smaller – and later outlawed – 'blast handle.'

During freefall the blast handle had tucked itself under my webbing. When it was time to pull, I could not find it. From the standard opening altitude of 2,500 feet, you have 12 seconds before impact. Twelve seconds to live or die. Twelve seconds to freeze or to do something.

I pulled my reserve handle and deployed the chest-mounted parachute. From my knothole it appeared to take an eternity to open. Ground observers said it was one of the quickest openings they had seen.

I made a hard landing on the pavement and Phil, one of the most strait-laced jumpers I ever knew, ran up to me and made sure I was uninjured.

"Congratulations, you saved yourself," he said as he pumped my hand furiously.

"What did you expect?" I replied.

"Well, you never know how someone is going to react when the pressure is on."

That night I had to buy my rigger[16] a case of beer. It taught me a deep lesson that action (or inaction) always has consequences. Most times these consequences are minor and trivial but doing nothing and trying to avoid a decision is a decision in itself.

Skydiving consumed our daylight hours, but the endless winds of the Great Plains often disrupted our plans. You could typically count on jumping till noon, taking a break during midday and getting one or two loads in before sunset.

Students could not jump during windy days, but some experienced jumpers chose to brave the forces of nature. The real issue was not with the main parachute, whose forward speed could approach 25 miles per hour and penetrate into the strong breeze, but rather with the limitations of the reserve.

These reserve parachutes were round, smaller in surface area and designed to get you down in a hurry. They offered minimal control, and landing under a reserve in high winds carried the real potential of serious injury.

---

[16]   A certified individual who is authorized to inspect, repack and re-certify emergency parachutes. In later years this rigger went on to pack parachutes for NASA's Space Shuttle program.

Once during a high-wind day, someone suggested it would be a good time to earn a cross-country patch.

"What's that?" I asked.

"Well," said the proponent, "you have to travel at least seven miles under canopy, so that means doing a hop-and-pop at 14,000 feet and letting the wind do the rest."

"Hum," I said. "What about the spot[17]? Where will we land?"

"Yeah, that's the tricky part," he concluded. "Because we don't really know how hard the upper-level winds are blowing, we'll take our best guess and probably get out about eight miles from the landing zone. That should be enough distance to get the cross-country."

Using the pretzel logic of '*it's too windy to jump so let's go jump*' we loaded up the plane and made our slow, slow climb[18] up to 14,000 feet.

Prior to loading up, I had taken the opportunity to roll a joint and stick it in my reserve pouch along with a book of matches.

Absolutely no one was aware of this activity. I figured it might be a once-in-a-lifetime opportunity to float around for up to 20 minutes, smoke a joint and take in the world. I also packed a cassette player featuring Led Zeppelin.

---

[17] The point over land at which you exit the aircraft. During normal jumping operations the spot is determined by throwing a weighted streamer out of the airplane from 2,500 feet and watching how far the air takes it before hitting the ground. This gives jumpers an idea of both wind speed and wind direction when under canopy. This wind drift calculation is used to determine the spot – or exit point - for all jumps during the day. The spot is always upwind from the landing zone, allowing jumpers to drift with the wind while aiming for the target.

[18] Non-turbo-charged airplanes begin to run out of steam around 9,500 feet. Beyond that altitude the planes might only climb at 300 feet per minute, making for a 35-minute ride up to our jump altitude.

We made our way heavenward and the earth kept getting smaller and smaller. This would be my highest altitude jump to date. Normally this altitude would allow for slightly more than one minute of freefall time, but in this case the idea was to jump out, stabilize your body and open immediately. We were so high that from the ground you could not even see the airplane with binoculars, let alone a tiny figure under canopy.

When it came my turn, I climbed out on the strut, assumed a standard student position and fell free of the aircraft. After about 5 seconds I pulled my ripcord and the parachute opened normally. Now for the fun part.

Reaching in my reserve pouch, I pulled out the joint and my matchbook. I struck the match and prepared to light up. But I had neglected to think about the air blowing over the match as I descended. The match blew out immediately upon striking. Okay, two matches at one time. Same deal - blown out immediately. Alright, 4 matches, here we go. No joy. Shit, shit, shit. Eight matches? Not going to happen.

In final desperation I grabbed the remaining matches into a single bundle, held the joint next to the strike strip and let loose. I sucked as the match bundle flared into life, giving me a hit of sulfur and successfully lighting up the slender joint. I put on Led Zeppelin and entered a state of real bliss while floating towards the target. It was an experience not replicated since.

As the minutes ticked down, the earth began to come into sharper focus. It was apparent that not only were our initial estimates off, but that the wind had gained additional speed while we were engaged in our little adventure. It was going to be a rough landing, a feet-butt-head landing in which the parachute immediately re-inflates and drags you to your death. Perhaps this was not such a great idea after all.

In these circumstances, all you can really do is face your parachute into the wind and make tiny corrections while the wind blows you ever backwards. We blew past the intended landing zone still at 1,000 feet, the earth rushing alarmingly beneath my legs. As the ground approached, I remembered my early training for the Parachute Landing Fall and brought my knees together, slightly bent.

I watched as one of my companions made a stand-up landing under his square canopy. He grinned widely as if to say *'look, I made it'* before the wind reinflated his canopy, jerked him violently backwards and swung his feet even with his head in a singular motion.

I landed as expected in a feet-butt-head position and immediately felt my chute begin to reinflate and catch the howling wind. I got drug on my back for a few seconds before releasing my canopy from the harness. No broken bones, no damage. All in all, a great success in my book.

The truck eventually located us one mile off course, and we hopped in the back for a ride back to the DZ. As I was off-loading my gear, one of the old jumpers approached me and blocked my path.

He was a Harley Davidson rider from back in the days with one good eye and a scar that ran diagonally across his chest from his waist to his shoulder blade. "My name is Bad Bob," he told me when we first met, "and I can't be killed. I laid down on the highway and let a semi run over me to prove it."

I thought this was a complete fabrication until two unimpeachable witnesses confirmed the very truth. They had watched bewildered as he laid down on the highway and let a semi run over him. Or maybe it was just one tire that grazed him, but the legend grew over time. Whatever it was, we knew in our heart of hearts that some part of it was true, and Bob's body bore witness in itself.

Another aspect to Bob-of-the-one-eye was his mystical nature. For many of us he felt like an oracle, some sort of netherworld being come up to spend time with mere mortals. He was more than a little ominous to me, and on occasion he would challenge us to 'low pull' contests.[19] He always won.

Bob continued to block my path as I angled toward the packing table. Looking me over hard with his one good eye he said, "I know what you were doing up there. I saw you."

"What are you talking about?" I protested.

---

[19] The ultimate game of chicken. Jump out of the airplane together and pass through the standard opening altitude of 2,500 feet without opening. Twelve seconds to eternity and counting. Continue falling. Now six seconds from eternity. Who is going to chicken out and pull first? Highly irresponsible and not endorsed by the safety officer.

"Up there, when you first opened up," he continued. "I saw you. You could hardly get that joint lit. I saw it all."[20]

The thing is, I believed him.

Once, a group of us took a field trip and visited a quasi-renegade drop zone whose training material was quite suspect. On the ground, students are taught by an instructor. In the air, students are supervised by a jumpmaster from the time they enter the aircraft until the time they exit. Once this duty is discharged, the jumpmaster often assumes the role of a normal skydiver and rides up to altitude with the rest of the load.

On this load the ground instructor was searching for someone – anyone – to act as jumpmaster for an ageing, judgment-impaired first jump student. I always had the impression that she and her husband had forced each other into this position during a drunken dare at the local gun-and-knife club.

I wisely declined to be the jumpmaster, having neither the legal designation nor the inclination to get involved. The ground instructor found a hapless skydiver to volunteer by offering to pay for his lift ticket.

As we took off, I could see slightly more than fear in this student's eyes. I saw what looked like deer-in-the-headlights unconsciousness. Not a good sign but the jumpmaster, who was seated behind the pilot, could not see her demeanor.

As we lined up on jump run and reached the exit point, the jumpmaster hooked up the static line, instructing her to climb out of the airplane and grab onto the strut. She did this without hesitation and waited for the jumpmaster's command.

20　Some of Bob's juju may have rubbed off on me once. We were standing on a roof with a St. Bernard down below, barking at us fiercely. *'SHUT UP'* I said to the dog in my mind. The dog quit barking, turned around and left. Bob looked over at me and asked, "How did you do that?" "I'm learning from you," I replied.

When he slapped her on the thigh and commanded "GO," she did not go. Nor did she look back at the jumpmaster and ask stupid rhetorical questions like I did on my first jump.

She just froze completely. Like a statue. Like Lot's wife turning into a pillar of salt. Like a dog on point. Like a Minnesota lake in early February with fish suspended in the ice.

"Fuck," said the jumpmaster as he looked at me. "What'll we do?"

"There is no we here," I shot back. "You are in charge. But maybe we can try to bring her back in."

By this time the pilot was getting involved. A human being hanging onto a wing strut creates a huge amount of drag, pulling the airplane down and to the right.

Pilots counteract this drag by lifting the wing up with aileron control and adding a bit of rudder. But all the time this drag wants to inevitably take the airplane on a downward trajectory.

"Get her off my strut," he yelled.

"Alright," said the jumpmaster and he handed me the static line.

Yelling into the prop blast, the hapless jumpmaster tried to get her attention. But she was catatonic and frozen solid, staring straight ahead. Both hands were wrapped in a death grip around the strut.

We were slowly losing altitude, and it was apparent that she was neither going to jump nor come back into the airplane of her own volition.

"What if we land with her?" he asked in a measure of desperation.

"Bad plan," I said as I envisioned her letting loose on final over the runway and splattering in full view of the spectators. "You got to dislodge her from the strut."

And so he began the long process of prying off fingers from the strut, one-by-one-by-one. In the meantime, the pilot was still fighting for control, unable to bank left or right for fear of stalling the aircraft. We motored northward at reduced power, now far away from the designated landing zone and heading ever closer towards the forbidden and dangerous landing zone of a rock quarry.

The jumpmaster stuck his head out the door of the aircraft and began prying her left hand from the strut. When he had dislodged all four fingers and a thumb, she pirouetted in the wind. I imagined her falling away from the plane as I held the static line loosely in my hand, but still she hung on.

Now he was forced to exit the aircraft as he began the extraction process on her right hand. An index finger released and still she resisted. Prying away her middle finger, she still maintained a death grip. Finally, he uncurled her ring finger and she fell free from the aircraft, static line deploying the parachute in a thankfully normal opening.

She landed in a remote field unharmed, and we drove out in a pickup to collect her. Arriving back at the airport I noted that somewhere in the process she had also deployed her front-mounted reserve parachute.

A little rattled and amazed at the ordeal, the jumpmaster asked her how the jump went.

"Oh, just fine," she said non-pulsed. "The opening was a little harder than I was expecting."

"This may not be the sport for you," I added, understanding that she had apparently blocked the entire episode from her consciousness.

"Yeah, my husband dared me," she confided to us. "I sure showed that bastard, didn't I?"

———————————

As if daytime excitement were not enough for the adrenaline junkies, at night the Milky Way presided over another level altogether.

The old base had a series of runways configured in a sort of X pattern. Two of these runways were almost 1.5 miles in length and 100 feet wide. They made for perfect high-speed runs and were utilized by the Police Academy, the Sports Car Club of America, our daytime skydiving operation, a regional sailplane group and drunken skydivers at night.

Thinking themselves immortal, skydivers at the DZ created several after-dark activities designed to test skill and courage. One of these night sports involved driving a van at 60 miles per hour down the runway while a pickup would run parallel to its path and close in. Jumpers would hop back and forth between the open van door and the pickup bed shouting *"Blue Sky, Black Death."*

On other nights Ralph, an older character hypothetically in charge of airport Crash and Rescue, would bring out the firetruck from below the control tower. He would load it up with skydivers and beer, turn the red lights on and allow a privileged few to ring the bell while racing down the deserted runway.

There were always numerous 'safety meetings' after dark, an inside joke at almost every drop zone I ever visited.

The United States Parachute Association (USPA) is a non-governmental organization put together to self-police the sport. Given the gypsy nature of its founding members, it was a lot like herding cats.

But despite the individualistic flavor of each drop zone, the USPA was able to adopt standard practices and safety protocols through the use of locally appointed Safety Officers.

Most Safety Officers took their obligations very seriously and would hold impromptu seminars and propose corrective action as the situation merited. The motto was always "Safety First."

It was only a matter of time before someone decided that drop zones should extend safety into the evening hours with *safety meetings*. These meetings were fully unsanctioned, completely unrelated to what the USPA had in mind and anything but safe.

The nexus of these meetings revolved around pot and alcohol, with the goal of getting very drunk and/or very high. A drinking game called "Cardinal Puff" was often associated with safety meetings. It was a memory game of increasing complexity where failed participants were required to take a beer shot. No one left the table sober.

The stated goal of all these activities was for the skydiver to feel 'safe.' When a fellow skydiver asked 'are you safe' what he really wanted to know was if your mind had been sufficiently blown; if you had reached your limits.

"I am safe" was most properly interpreted as "I am so wasted that I can hardly see straight."

In that way, both by day and by night, the skydiving community was able to develop a deep and abiding respect for safety.

———————

One of the greatest paradoxes of the DZ was its physical location less than 100 yards away from the state's only law enforcement training academy. Local police from all over the state would come here, spend weeks in training, take classes on forensic analysis, practice on the live-fire range, and learn high-speed driving techniques[21] on the abandoned 10,000-foot runways.

What was even more paradoxical was their lack of policing powers while at the academy. Because these were city cops in training, they were completely removed from their local jurisdiction and unable to enforce the law. Any law.

The kind of laws that, back in their local jurisdiction, would have landed every one of us in the county jail for 30 days. Things that the skydiving crowd considered normal behavior, such as smoking pot, driving on the runway while intoxicated, public urination, underage drinking and a host of

---

[21]   We used their same road course on the weekends, practicing both inattentive driving and DUI at the same time. If cell phones existed back then, we surely would have been talking and texting as well.

other violations. Our motto was that it was all just fun and games as long as no one got hurt.

Some of these activities were easily visible by our neighbors next door and yet remained unenforceable. For a bunch of castaways and social outcasts, it was nirvana. Sometimes we would drive by in our pickup and hoist a beer in a sort of mock salute while they watched in silent anger. I suspect they were hoping from time to time that one of us would bounce.[22]

But perhaps the most ironic aspect of it all was a personal war between myself and a local police officer that had bound us together in my hometown and followed us, almost by divine appointment, to the DZ.

It all started a few years earlier with a gross misunderstanding back in my hometown. My buddies and I had been riding around in my mom's car, smoking pot and pretending she wouldn't notice the smell on her crushed velour seats the next day.

Scott had been particularly stoned in the backseat and let a small bag of pot escape from his jacket before passing out. When he came to, we were in a parking lot full of rednecks itching for a fight. Scott was game, while I – ever the peacemaker – tried to cool the situation down. Scott finally stumbled off to his car, drove over an impressive array of high curbs and disappeared into the night just as the police arrived.

Cops being cops, they got out their flashlights and began waving them around. They came over to my car and spotted Scott's bag in the back seat about the same time I did. Shit! It didn't take a genius to see how this was going to end.

Roger Ramjet, the newly hired rookie cop, got excited as he looked at me across the wide expanse of the car's roof line.

"Name?" he demanded with the flashlight beam blinding my eyes. I gave it to him. "Address?" came the next query and I recited it. "Date of birth?" he asked.

---

[22] A colloquial term explaining the physics of a skydiver's body hitting the earth at 120 mph when a parachute fails to open. At impact, the body typically bounces upward approximately three feet before settling back onto terra firma and eternal rest.

About this time, I, having seen all the police shows on TV, decided I had volunteered enough information.

"It's on the license," I said as I tossed my identification in his direction over the roof.

"I said what's your date of birth?" Roger demanded in a rising tone.

"And I said it's on the license," I answered, beginning to visualize room and board down at the city jail.

About that time the other cop walked up. He was my mom's second cousin[23]. He took the tiny bag of pot, dumped it in the street and assessed the situation between me, the rednecks and a growing crowd of interested spectators.

"Alright everybody, the show's over. Get out of here and go home," he offered in an Andy Griffith sort of move. We all dispersed, and I thanked God for getting me out of a tight spot.

But Officer Ramjet was not thanking God. In fact, he began a systematic harassment campaign that bordered on the absurd. He even got the sheriff involved. How do I know? The sheriff's son, a pot-smoking friend of mine, told me.

"My dad's out to get you," he said one night. "You better be careful."

My response? I bought a pack of Zigzags, typically used exclusively for pot, and rolled Uncle Albert tobacco into suspicious-looking joints. These I placed on the dash of my car and waited for Officer Ramjet to stop me. Which he did one night at a local convenience store.

After calling in for backup, a smarter officer realized it was tobacco and they let me go. Score: 2-to-0.

He stopped me one night for executing a U-turn which he said was illegal. I quoted his own rule book back to him and he had to let me go. Score now 3-to-0.

---

[23] Forget what I was thinking about close-relation-breeding in small town America. At times it can be very beneficial.

Soon after that I left town and moved into a small corner of the DZ's gigantic barracks.

While living there, I found a part-time opportunity next door, slinging hash at the Law Enforcement Training Academy's cafeteria. One day Roger Ramjet entered the line and headed in my direction. I recognized him instantly, but it took him a bit longer before he realized who I was.

"What are you doing here?" he said shaking his head in a sort of shocked disbelief.

"Feeding you," I replied as I hacked a fake cough in the back of my throat and handed him the lunch tray. Score now 4-to-0.

In one last irony, the next year I was back at our local radio station, working as a Disc Jockey during the night shift. A guy called up, introduced himself as a member of a local county and western band and asked if he could drop off a demo tape for the station manager.

I told him to ring the doorbell and I would collect it. About ten minutes later the doorbell rang. When I opened it, there stood Roger Ramjet, out of uniform but open-mouthed. "You again?" he said in disbelief. I took his tape, shut the door and deposited it on the manager's desk. Score: 5-to-0.

A Confession:

I would like to end this story at the radio station and proclaim victory, but that's not ultimately how it ended. About three months later I found myself cruising down Main Street with three friends, stuffed in the back of a poorly designed but aptly named AMC Gremlin compact car.

It was well past Midnight, and as one of the town elders once proclaimed to his wayward son, "there ain't nothing good happens after midnight."

Roger Ramjet was cruising the streets, met us in oncoming traffic, whipped a U-turn and pulled in behind us. As was standard operating procedure at the time, we were stoned, having just broken in a new, high-priced bong. I'm pretty sure there was smoke rolling out the windows as the red lights came on.

"Shit" said Darryl as he looked out the rear window at impending doom. "What'll I do with the bong?"

Someone suggested stashing it under the front seat. When it wouldn't fit, an alternate plan was suggested to smash it into little pieces. Darryl-of-the-big-feet began furiously stomping the acrylic wonder, causing the car's inadequate suspension to sway back and forth.

Officer Ramjet strolled up to the driver's window.

"You didn't use your turn signal back there," he said. "That's why I'm stopping you."

But as his flashlight scanned the back seat, he spotted his great adversary; he a sort of crazed Captain Ahab and I, his Moby Dick. Instead of asking the driver for his license, he went straight for me.

"Name?" he demanded as he shined the flashlight in my eyes. I gave it to him. "Address?" came the next query and I recited it. "Date of birth?" he asked.

Here was the moment of truth, the tilting of the scales, the final act, the mano e mano confrontation. Would I bow down to his authoritarianism? Would I submit? A lot was hanging on this moment.

I gave him my date of birth. He looked satisfied and removed the bright beam from my face. He had finally won.

"Okay, you boys can go," he said. "Next time, remember to use your turn signal[24]."

We pulled away and Darryl looked at me. "What the fuck was that about? I just destroyed my new bong."

"I'm sure I have no idea," I said lying through my teeth.

---

[24] From personal observation here in Central Florida, most 4-wheel-drive diesel trucks appear to have inoperative turn signals. Roger Ramjet could come down here, settle down around Kissimmee or St. Cloud, and make a fortune issuing tickets.

Yet it was impossible not to hear lines from an old song running through my head: "*I fought the law and . . . . . the law won. I fought the law and the law won.*"

A Final DZ Story

One of the side jobs I snagged at the DZ that summer was insulating houses with a new expanding foam[25] that promised to slash energy bills. My boss purchased a very expensive system that mixed the chemicals inside a big box truck and pumped them under high pressure to a hand nozzle.

This nozzle was inserted between the studs of exterior walls and filled up the cavity with an expanding foam. It took a practiced hand to sense when to shut off the nozzle. At the time, most home foam companies were boring three-inch holes directly through the exterior walls of homes before inserting the nozzle.

When finished, they would use a round plastic plug to reseal the opening. It was quick and effective, but really destroyed the aesthetic of many a fine home and left hundreds of ugly 'butt plugs' spaced every 24 inches apart.

My boss hated this look and would carefully lift and remove lap siding from each row around the house before drilling holes. After applying the foam, we would use the same plastic plug to seal the job but would then reattach existing siding. This attention to detail brought in more business than we could handle.

The boss let me operate the nozzle only one time. We were working in an upscale neighborhood, and I dragged the hose up with me to a second story landing. Looking over the vista, I imagined myself as Zeus, the King of Everything and Lord Father of All.

---

[25] There was a slight problem with the first generation of this foam. It used formaldehyde as a drying agent, and as a result, we may have been inducing a few unintended medical consequences. It took a while to understand why the customers, enjoying their newly insulated home and lower utility bills, always wanted to sleep. It turns out they were being slowly pickled by the formaldehyde fumes.

I put the nozzle between my legs and opened the valve. Vast quantities of foam ejaculated out from the nozzle, spewing a never-ending arc of white fluid through the air.

My boss shook his head in silent disbelief. Only the mind of a seventeen-year-old could envision such a thing.

Aside from my immaturity, there was a real art form involved in operating the valve. Because you could not visually see how much foam was entering the cavity, it required a sort of Zen awareness. Too little foam meant an ineffective seal. Too much foam could result in walls popping free of the studs, causing cosmetic and potential structural damage inside the home.

One time we were foaming a Catholic church with a very high and steeply pitched roof. Cavities rose more than 40 feet from the ground to the peak. The boss was trying to feel his way through this job and could not easily determine when to shut the nozzle off. He asked me to go inside and check.

I went through the back door and arrived at the alter concurrent with the cleaning lady.

"Holy Mary, Mother of God" she screamed as a torrent of foam flew over Jesus' left shoulder and onto the alter.

"Shut it off," I yelled as I ran out the door, my hands exhibiting that universal throat-slashing gesture.

The priest and my boss walked in at the same time to survey the damage. Because the foam was super-sticky, it was imperative that we (I) start cleaning the altar immediately.

"Are you sure this is okay?" I asked, thinking about my retreating Protestant faith and the eternal consequences of standing shoulder to shoulder with Jesus on a Catholic alter.

"Just be quick," said the priest. "And make sure you clean up Mary as well."

———————

In retrospect, this fun and crazy period in my life may have knocked my moral compass off a point or two.

It may have allowed some ideas to enter my mind that heretofore were off limits, suggesting some forms of employment that had not been discussed by my high school counselors. These were seeds that had been planted, and they were growing wild without the need for much water.

It had been a mind-blowing and enlightening summer, but it was time to get more serious and head off to my freshman year at the big university.

The Long and Winding Road

In small towns all over America, the road after high school graduation seemed to bifurcate sharply. The locals tended to stay put, find jobs, get married and have children early on. The other group packed up and left town, many of us never to return.

My group left for college, bound primarily for either the land grant college at Manhattan or Snob Hill (the University of Kansas). I opted for snob hill and spent one decade in pursuit of an eventual degree.

In the larger world of the university, I was marginally prepared to study, and unable to attract so much as a wink from our former small-town girlfriends. They had gone on to greener pastures with the Kansas City boys, and it took a while to understand the dynamics and why we didn't have a card to play.

Like an engine's timing belt that slips a notch, all the male/female dynamics had slid one cog. The Kansas City boys were dating the small-town girls. Why? Because the Kansas City girls were dating the St. Louis Boys. Why was this? Because the St. Louis girls had upgraded to dating Chicago boys.

Who knows what else the Chicago boys were doing? Perhaps dating themselves. But at the very bottom of the rung remained small town Kansas boys, unable to impress anyone. We even scouted the high schools in hopes of a date, but these girls were mostly the daughters of university professors and certainly not impressed by how far we could spit tobacco.

The small-town boys were forced to run solo with each other, commiserating our bad misfortune, lying about our age to facilitate drinking binges and telling ourselves that involuntary celibacy was a stage we would quickly pass through once our former flames regained their senses. We played Johnny River's *Poor Side of Town* over and over in our heads.

"How can you tell me how much you miss me, when the last time I saw you, you wouldn't even kiss me? That rich guy you've been seeing must have put you down, so welcome back baby to the poor side of town."

Pride and self-delusion are funny things. I would often watch sorority girls go by who imagined themselves as Bo Derrick from the movie "10". I would dream that I was somehow desirable in their eyes. Occasionally, my eyes would light upon a girl whom I imagined could be my perfect mate.[26]

During one of my academic absences, I moved to southern California and took advantage of my brother's offer of a free room. It was there, roaming about the San Diego coast in his restored 1965 Le Mans convertible[27], that I encountered the honest to goodness '10s of SoCal'. I had never seen such beauty; certainly not at Snob Hill and certainly not with so little clothing.

I would hang out at Pacific Beach and engage in my favorite people watching activities. I would spend time at La Jolla, looking out over its magnificent cliffs and westward across the gorgeous Pacific Ocean.

On one rather bold (and alcohol-fueled day) I even ventured onto a nude beach. But above it all were the stunningly beautiful girls of Southern California. With perfect bodies and flawless skin, it made me think that perhaps some close relative breeding had been occurring back in the Midwest.

---

[26] For many years I held in my mind this notion that when 'The One' came I would know her by some sort of cosmic sign. Once, sitting in the Student Union and eating lunch, my eye fell upon an unusually attractive girl. Almost immediately my crotch began to warm up. "Wow," I thought, "that's interesting. She could be The One."

As I continued to watch her, my crotch kept heating up. It began to get warm. Then it got really warm. Then it got hot. Then it got damn hot. Then it got skin-burning hot. 'Shit,' I thought as I reached into my pocket for further investigation. What I found was that a nine-volt battery had come into contact with an errant penny, creating a sort of mini nuclear power plant thermal runaway event. I yanked the battery out from my pocket as the girl walked away.

I guess the lesson I learned was to be careful of how you interpret signs from above.

[27] Beneath a stock exterior, he had replaced the anemic 326 engine with a 455 cubic inch monster motor. Driving down the I-5 one night I smoked an unsuspecting GTO. It was fast and it was fun.

When I returned home to continue my studies, I had a different perspective on beauty. As the Snob Hill girls would pass by, trying to exude their false and haughty air of superiority, I would nod and say silently to my own satisfaction: *"You are a 7.214, not a 10, and only because I am a very generous guy. Lay off the corn."*

I would be painting a false picture of my university days if I portrayed them as gloomy. On the contrary I have brilliant memories from that time: laying under intense azure skies beneath the library's magnificent oaks, having illuminating discussions in the philosophy department, making a wrong turn in the music department and hearing a men's group practicing *My Funny Valentine*, a girlfriend now and then, Iranian students getting hauled off to FBI headquarters, my friend Randy and I flying down New Hampshire Street in his Datsun 280Z with police in hot pursuit, and of course the endless parties.

At the time I entered college, Kansas had an open admission policy. You didn't have to take an ACT test or achieve a particular score to attend one of the state's seven colleges. You just had to be a resident, have some folding money in your pocket and show proof of recent high school graduation.

To my way of thinking there was an additional requirement, and it was measured by how much alcohol you could consume. On that scale I passed with flying colors.

For those of a particular mindset, the parties at Lawrence were epic and endless. Sometimes the dormitories would allow for a keg or two of beer, and hundreds of students would test the structural limit of the concrete floors.

Other times you would be driving down the street and notice people pouring out of dilapidated houses in what was accurately referred to as 'the student slums.' This was a particular part of town located near the campus and given to high rent, chronic student over-crowding and landlords who only seemed to appear on the first of every month.

If you had good enough social skills, you could partake of OPB (other people's beer) and make a new friend or two.

There were of course fraternity and sorority parties with their ever-present allegations of hazing and their trophy girls from the Kansas City suburbs.

But as a sworn enemy of the Greek system, I never found my groove around this crowd. Of course, much to my dismay, this interconnected web of undesirables later came to run the county, the state, the federal government and the World Economic Forum.

There were endless apartment parties, and lots of rich foreign students from Columbia with questionable financial backing. At one such party I met David, and we talked about rock-and-roll groups.

He was astounded that I had never heard of the group Jes. It was only when he spelled out the name Y-E-S that I said "Yes, of course I know this group." And as if to solidify our shared understanding, he said "Jes."

There was even a gigantic Catholic life center that held parties from time to time. As a backslidden Lutheran, I remember the shame of being caught one night by my pastor.

We inadvertently ran into each other at a local bar. Neither one of us could conjure up a good reason for being there, so we managed a sort of unspoken truce in the months that followed.

But here in Lawrence the priest was knocking them back, smoking a big cigar and generally having a much better time than protestants were allowed to think about. For a while it moved my needle toward converting to Catholicism.

I remember falling in love with a beautifully sculptured long blond one night. I talked to her and was convinced she might be the one. But as the night and alcohol wore on, an unexpected and deeply ugly side poured out of her. It taught me a lesson that beauty may only be skin deep, but ugly goes clean through to the soul.

And it was at one such party that I met Vince, who in a few years would invite me into a whole other world.

Like me, Vince was from a small Midwest town and had managed to get hooked up with some Chicago dealers. They may or may not have been Mafia. I never knew and never asked, but I had my suspicions. They lived upstairs in the same apartment complex as I did, and their loud music was an instant invitation to come and make introductions.

Vince and I became good friends, listened to Genesis at obnoxious volumes, and partook of that most sacred and intimate act of the era – smoking pot out of a bong.[28]

Like much of the drug dealing in college towns, there was a certain hierarchy involved. Your roommate might be buying a quarter pound of pot and splitting it up into one-ounce bags. These bags might get further sub-divided into 'dimes,' an antiquated notion by which you could purchase an amount of pot for $10. This was low level, down-stream distribution stuff.

Vince occupied a middle rung of the ladder, taking 20-pound shipments from the Chicago team, dividing them into one-pound bags and selling them downstream.

---

[28]   My early college days were funded by what I presumed to be an endless parental endowment. I lived in a private apartment, drove an MGB and floated in-and-out of academic probation. This came to a crashing end when my parents made a surprise visit to my luxury apartment. I had just said goodbye to a couple of friends after a marathon bong session when the doorbell rang.

Thinking it was my just-departed friends, I opened the door to find my parents standing at the threshold. They invited themselves in. As hard as I tried to steer them out of the kitchen, they kept moving in that direction and towards my prominent bong. Spying the foreign object, my mom pointed and asked what it was. "A bong," I said. "A whaattt?" she asked with deep foreboding. "A bong," I repeated. And I spelled it out for her. B-O-N-G.

"Is it for smoking marijuana?" she asked in a stuttering voice. When I affirmed its purpose, she became angry (or perhaps just profoundly disappointed). My dad, with significant hearing loss from his WWII bomber experience, picked up very little of the conversation but every bit of my mom's anger. They left in a huff. What a major screw up on my part.

But there was an upstream hierarchy as well. Somebody was buying 100 pounds at a time, and somebody else was buying pot by the truck load. Somebody upstream from them was buying boatloads (or planeloads) of pot, and it was a never-ending cycle that needed a distribution system.

By this time in my academic life, I was running with a suspect crowd, doing poorly in school and continuing to skydive on the weekends. Coming and going from the university would prove to be a long-term pattern in my life, so when the Dean sent me a personal letter - asking me not to return for a semester or two - I was happy to oblige.

Birth Of An Aviator

I was 20 years old, free from the constraints of academia and still jumping. I had exchanged the cheapo for a mostly state of the art Jalbert Parafoil, owned a jumpsuit that allowed me to fly with surprising control, and had accumulated more than 300 skydives. I was not a skygod, but I had learned to control my body with a great deal of precision.

To support this habit, I turned my high school passion into a paying career, working for a couple of daily newspapers as a photographer. But to be fair to the industry, daily newspapers paid poverty wages. I was getting the itch to become a pilot and knew I needed a better paying job.

One of my high school friends had managed to work his way into the aircraft manufacturing sector. I called to see if he could find a position for me.

With a little luck and a lot of pull, I snagged a job towing and fueling corporate jets. It felt like a huge step toward my goal of flying - at least until the first few paychecks arrived. Uncle Sam was taking his cut and inflation during that time was brutal.

If I was going to afford flying lessons, I needed a second job. God and the universe generously provided me with a night position, fueling and towing much smaller piston engine airplanes at a nearby FBO.

This job would turn out to be pivotal, giving rise to Bill Mahoney and providing for a new level of insanity that eclipsed anything I had experienced in the skydiving world.

"You want to go flying?" asked the flight instructor as we talked about my upcoming first flying lesson.

"Yes," I said, "I want to become a pilot."

"Alright, let's go out and bore a few holes in the sky."

We headed out on the tarmac, fighting the brutal Midwest sun and the ever-present southern wind. The Central Plains remain a great mixing bowl of weather systems; winds howling eastward over the Rockies, moist air driving north from the Gulf, and cold air flowing south from Canada.

The net result of these converging systems gives the Central Plains an ever-changing weather pattern and the unfortunate moniker of tornado alley. Mobile home parks are unofficially known as tornado magnets and there is even a local drink called a Titty Twister.

As a result, it's always windy on the Plains and a challenge to flight. The smaller the airplane the greater the wind's effect, and ultra-light fliers must pick and choose the days they launch their tiny kites into the air with great care.

As my instructor approached the Cessna 150, he began a slow and methodical lecture about airplane safety and the importance of inspection before each flight. As we reached the aircraft, he opened the thin door and pulled out a checklist.

"This is important stuff," he said handing me the Pre-Flight Checklist. We made a clockwise circle around the aircraft, checking this and that, wiggling control surfaces and climbing up on the wing to visually check the fuel tanks. When he was satisfied the craft was fit for flight, he opened the left door, inviting me to climb into the pilot's seat.

The first thing that struck me was the tiny nature of this two-seat flying machine. First introduced in 1959, it retained its basic shape and function for more than 25 years. It made me wonder if pilots were smaller back then, because when the instructor got in and shut his door, we were shoulder-to-shoulder.

In this light-weight trainer, I got my first lesson in aircraft design, and it is that weight is a killer. An engineer's job is not to make the strongest airframe possible but rather the lightest airframe possible that will meet the strength requirements.

The earliest builders knew this when airplanes were made of wood. They identified and located a unique species along the coast of Alaska. This Sitka Spruce was not the strongest wood available, but rather it was the wood with the highest strength-to-weight ratio. And it became the de facto building material until a better replacement (aluminum) was introduced 20 years later.

Even today this is the challenge for aircraft companies when they introduce a new model. In order to fly so many miles with so many passengers and burn so much fuel, an aircraft must meet tightly defined weight targets established early in the design phase. Weekly meetings are held in which every engineering department accounts for every ounce of every part.[29]

We started the engine and obtained permission to taxi away from our location on the ramp.

"Want to steer her?" he asked. "It's not like a car and you don't use the control wheel for......"

"I know," I interrupted. "You use the rudder pedals to steer and apply brakes if you need to. The control column is linked to the elevators and the ailerons."

"Okay," he said obviously impressed. "It's all yours. Let's see if you can manage to get us to the runway."

I maneuvered down the apron while he worked the radios. Near the end of the taxiway, he turned the airplane into the wind and did a run-up, checking to make sure the engine was operating properly and making full power. Scanning the gauges, we confirmed that all systems were operating normally.

With that, he contacted the tower and received permission to enter the active runway.

---

[29]   Some of the most intense meetings I attended were design reviews for new aircraft, and the heated exchanges that occurred from time to time as various disciplines were called on the carpet for busting their weight targets.

"Want to try a takeoff?" he asked in his best nothing-can-rattle-me tone.[30]

"The idea is to use the rudder pedals, and with gentle corrections, keep the nose on the center line while we gain speed. I'll handle the yoke and lift us off when we reach 70. Are you game?"

I affirmed and moved the throttle gently forward to its full stop. Everything in an airplane is logical, and all manufacturers have adopted this standard design logic.

If you want more of anything you move the levers forward. If you want flaps or landing gear, the levers and switches go up or down. If you want to use fuel from one wing tank or another, a selector lever points toward the respective tank.

This standardization extends into the pilot's handbook as well. Pick up a book from any of the small airplane manufacturers and you will instantly feel at home. It's a sparse language with no flowery adjectives hanging around the nouns or verbs. Sort of like the shortest verse in the bible.[31]

---

[30] The best flight instructors are stellar human beings. On one hand their job is to install a sense of calm and confidence while you begin to master a whole new skill set. Think of them as Driver's Ed instructors on steroids. On the other hand - and this is constantly running thru the back of their minds - is a certain knowledge that student pilots have absolutely no idea what they are doing. In this environment, a student's bone-headed actions could well jeopardize life and limb without much advance warning.

They breathe deeply while their cat-like reflexes are ready to spring into action and take back control at any second. Their declarative statement of "I've got it" is a command for you to relinquish control of the aircraft. What they are really conveying is this: *'Quit it, you stupid son of a bitch. You are going to kill us all. Get your hands and feet off the controls right now so I can rectify your mistakes and keep us alive and flying!'*

[31] "Jesus wept." John 11:35.

If you delve into the radio language between aircraft controllers and pilots, you will likewise hear abbreviated speech. All business and no chatter. *"Six-eight Zulu, turn right heading two-four-zero contact center one-two-four-point-eight"* is a command for an aircraft whose identification ends in 68Z to make an immediate right turn to a compass heading of 240°, dial in a new radio frequency of 124.8 MHz and announce their position to a different controller.

Pilots are required to repeat these instructions and listen for the response *'read-back correct.'* In heavy traffic areas it takes a keen ear to hear your specific instructions, as controllers spit out dozens of messages to dozens of aircraft all maneuvering in the same airspace at the same time.

As we rolled down the runway, I kept the nose directly over the center line while my instructor called out the airspeed in increasing numbers.

"Forty, 50, 60, 65 and rotation" he said as we lifted off the runway and began a shallow climb, still keeping on track with the runway below us.

When clear of the runway we received instructions from the tower: *'Six-eight Zulu, turn left heading two-seven-zero cleared three five hundred to the practice area.'*

"Want to take the controls?" he asked, and I nodded in the affirmative.

"You've got the airplane" he replied, taking his hands off the yoke.

I brought a true and steady hand to the machine, and he was visibly impressed. He began to introduce an increasingly complex series of maneuvers which he would ask me to perform. I complied with precision.

After about 45 minutes he looked over at me.

"You sure you've never flown before? You are the most natural-born pilot I have ever taught. I have never had a student like you. Now let's start our descent."

"I don't know what to do," I volunteered.

"What do you mean?" he asked in a perplexed voice. "You said you have been up in an airplane 300 times."

"Yes, but I've always jumped out at the top. I have never landed in an airplane and have no idea what goes on from here"[32].

It took me a long time to get the hang of descent and landing, mostly because I had never experienced it before. At the top of the learning curve was understanding how to treat engines and not let them cool too fast during descent.

The motors of small airplanes are ancient in design and find their nexus almost 70 years in the past. They are, almost without exception, air-cooled, opposed cylinders (think VW Beetle, Subaru Outback or Porsche 911) and fire the spark plugs with old-style magnetos that disappeared from car design in the 1920s.

There are a myriad of reasons why this ancient design is still around. At the top of the list is reliability. A sort of 'if it ain't broke don't fix it' mentality. Next in line is a highly regulatory environment in which each and every part has a birth certificate attached to it. This goes so far as to include nuts, bolts, rivets, sealer and a thousand things you would never think could be traced.

---

[32]   Two years ago, there was a 'non-pilot makes miracle landing story' floating around the national news circuit. It was like God had given this man a jolt of superman power as he heroically wrestled with the unknown, finally bringing an out-of-control ship safely to the ground while the pilot lay slumped and unconscious.

It turns out this non pilot superman hero had sat up front for ten years, watching his friend fly the very airplane he so miraculously landed. Much like me, this guy had watched and learned some of the basic motor skills required to fly. I wasn't a natural born pilot as much as a good observer.

This speaks to the value of observation and how knowledge can get transferred subconsciously.

But perhaps overriding all these factors is the tiny, tiny number of aircraft related parts manufactured each year. These small numbers result in an obscenely high price-per-unit cost[33].

Toyota once came to town, hired as a consultant. They offered many excellent ideas to improve plant efficiency but were astounded that we were still building jets by hand. The consultant spent a great deal of time talking about the automation involved with their best-selling Camry.

"How many cars did you build last year?" asked a Manufacturing Engineer who had been the object of much Japanese scorn and derision.

"500,000," said the Toyota consultant with pride. "How many jets did you build last year?"

"Twenty," came the even response.

I learned about engines, how to read temperature probes, how to change the fuel-to-air ratio, how to request altitude changes from controllers, why a carburetor would freeze over in the middle of summer, how to read a sectional map and a million other small things associated with flying. In short, I was becoming a pilot, even if it was in an insignificant little two-seater.[34]

---

[33]   Well, there's another thing. The industry has always enjoyed making truckloads of money. Once, while specing out his jet, a customer balked at the price of adding wood and special plating to his interior. "How in good conscience can you charge me $60,000 for a little wood and plating?" he demanded. I looked at him square in the eyes. "Well, both my kids are in private schools." He exploded in laughter. "Finally," he said, "somebody willing to tell the truth. I have to respect that. Put it on order."

[34]   Once while deplaning from a commercial airliner, I thanked the captain for the flight. He noticed the wings attached to my leather jacket. When asked, I told him I was 'just' a private pilot. "Son," he said with a smile, "don't ever apologize for being a pilot. There are only two kinds of people in the world, and you are one of us."

As my flight time grew so did my confidence. Lesson after lesson I moved forward towards that most monumental of student achievements, the Solo flight.

It's a time – the first time in the history of the entire world – when you leave earth without an instructor. Although it's a widely anticipated milestone, it always comes as a shock when your mentor gets out of the plane and says, "okay, it's all yours."

This is about as full-spectrum sensory overload as it gets. Elation, fear, excitement, self-doubt, pride, sweaty palms, a slight tremor of the hands and shallow breaths until a calmer spirit prevails. It is certainly up there at some level with the first time you make love.

Taxing out, it's you on the radio talking to controllers. It's you making sure the engine output is 100 percent. Hands on the throttle, it's you moving down the runway and looking at the airspeed, feeling the ship get lighter and lighter.

Most surprising of all is the way the airplane leaps off the runway. The anemic trainer that often struggles to climb at more than 500 feet per minute with an instructor suddenly feels like a fighter jet. All your expectations about performance must be rethought, and there is no one beside you to help figure it out.

Maybe this is how a baby bird feels when mom pushes her out of the nest and requires it to either fly or die[35].

---

[35] Here's a funny story (or not), depending on your perspective. For the first 25 years of my life, I had a sort of revolving door at my parent's house. With a separate entrance above a garage room, it was like having a subsidized lifestyle; an endlessly available Airbnb with charges that never appeared on my credit card.

"It's nice to have you back again," my mom said as I made my way up the familiar stairs. And then as if to finish her thought she added "for the last time." To this day she has no memory of the conversation while I retain a certain impression of getting kicked out of the nest, flapping furiously and hoping to god those wings would unfold before I hit the ground.

As I cleared the runway I spoke to the tower and told them I would be staying in the pattern, doing touch-and-goes.

It's a routine in which practice makes perfect. Full power for a couple of minutes, stabilizing your altitude at 1,200 feet then a gentle bank to the left. Controlling your airspeed, reducing power just a bit, watching your altimeter and establishing base leg. Think of it like an extended oval racetrack, running in a counterclockwise direction.

As you fly on the downwind leg, parallel to the runway but offset a half mile and traveling in the opposite direction of takeoff, it's time for GUMP.

Gas – Fuel selector on Both
Undercarriage – Down and Locked
Mixture – Rich
Prop – Full

It is a universal acronym that helps pilots avoid the most egregious landing error, forgetting to put the gear down. It happens more times than rationality might suggest.

In it all is this idea of gentleness and a soft touch – no jerky, last-minute jinxing of the controls. Everything smooth. A gentle reduction in power, carb heat on, slowing the airplane down to 80 miles per hour, watching the tachometer at 1,500 rpm. Seeing the runway now behind you and over your left shoulder, you make another gentle bank, losing altitude, reducing power again and entering base.

Then, if you've flown your pattern correctly, a final left turn as the runway appears on your nose, and you announce 'on final' to the tower. Power back to near-idle as you come in. It's here in the netherworld between sky and earth that bliss can overtake you. Gentle; steady; steady; only minor movements[36] to the controls.

---

36   Sometimes, when it is windy and gusty during a landing, the complete opposite is true. You will be set up perfectly to land, and a gust of wind will change everything. It takes super-fast reflexes to restore the airplane's attitude. The slower you go during this final phrase, the more radical the control input must be. On these days, landing is not a joyful act but more closely resembles a sword fight.

Then over the numbers, airspeed decreasing, decreasing, decreasing as you keep the plane slightly off the runway like a duck coming down over the water and hovering, as if suspended in time.

Finally, as you end the bliss, a chirp of the tires as they spin up from zero to 60 in a second. No longer a bird, but merely a thing with wheels and long, long arms.

When you taxi in, the instructor meets you with a pair of scissors. Not to stab you in the eye, but to cut off your shirt tail. The origins of this tradition are murky but well established. Most flight schools around the world have a room to display these tokens of first solo, complete with student name and date of the milestone.

It's tough luck if you didn't anticipate the solo and wore your best Ralph Lauren. It's getting cut up to join its brothers and sisters on the wall of fame.

From here on out training takes on a building block approach, one new skill reinforcing the previous lessons. I learned how to fly using instruments and how the earth's magnetic field tricks pilots into flying off course.

The hours continued to accrue in my logbook, alternating between acquiring new skills with my instructor and practicing those skills as a solo pilot. The regulations limit the distance you can fly from your home airport, and near the end of my training I was signed off to make a long cross-country flight.

This triangular flight would require me to fly at least 90 miles in one direction before landing. At that airport I would get someone to sign my logbook and take off for the second leg, also at least 90 miles distant. With another signature in hand, it would be back to the home airport.

These flights were designed to bring together all the learned skills; communicating with air traffic control and other pilots, using radio navigation aids, learning to interpret the sectional chart with terrain below and - most important of all - fuel management.

Somehow, I failed the last lesson and managed to run my airplane out of gas within sight of the home airport.

I could try and paint a more favorable picture of my actions, but the facts tell a different story.

As a student pilot working low-paying day and night jobs, money was tight. Despite having a roommate, we could ill afford to run the window air conditioning unit during the hottest summer on record. I ate beans and rice, with all excess funds going towards my flying expenses.

My lack of income disqualified me from obtaining a credit card. When the instructor asked if I had enough cash money to refill the plane at its second leg, I affirmed I did.

And I might have just made it home with the minimum fuel reserves (30 minutes of flight time) had I not elected to see how high the airplane could fly.

When flying on a VFR (visual flight rules) flight plan in uncontrolled airspace, pilots have a wide latitude to change altitude. Perhaps remembering my cross-country skydiving adventure, I elected to take the airplane from its flight-planned altitude of 4,500 feet up to 14,000 feet.

I was able to coax the airplane to this height but only by consuming large amounts of fuel that I did not have. Staying at this altitude for some time, I noted how small and insignificant the earth appeared below my wings.

Flying at such height alters your perspective. The plane becomes the one fixed reference point, and the earth appears to be rotating underneath. Pearl S. Buck captured this feeling in her 1930s book *The Good Earth* where it was the oxen's feet that were slowly turning the earth.

I began to drop from this altitude, doing so slowly and without haste, remembering from my earlier instruction that diving too fast can over-cool the engine[37] and cause damage. In this way I eventually returned to my 4,500-foot altitude and began the final 40-mile approach to my home airport.

---

[37] Shock cooling.

As I got within striking distance of the airport, I kept looking at the fuel gauges, trying to convince myself they were inaccurate. They both appeared to be stuck on 'E' despite vigorous wagging of the wings.

There were smaller airports underneath my wing, but with no cash and no credit cards I could not buy fuel. It would be embarrassing to call my instructor and ask him to drive over with credit cards and refuel the aircraft so close to home. Surely there was sufficient fuel to make it back.

When examining crashes, air safety investigators often cite the almost-universal *accident chain*. It's not one thing that causes an accident, but rather a series of bad decisions made one after another that result in an inevitable outcome.

With ten miles to go before landing, I began to relax a bit. A close shave, a stupid mental error but nothing more.

"Six-eight Zulu, switch to Tower one-two-four-point-eight," the controller said. And then adding that extra word sometimes allowed in the lingo, *"good day."*

I announced my position on the tower frequency and listened to the ever-present chatter between pilots and controller as airplanes converged and departed in a ballet of controlled chaos. Traveling over the city center at 100 miles per hour and five miles out, I was breathing a sigh of relief when the engine consumed its last ounce of fuel, sputtered for 30 seconds and then died.

There is an old joke about what function the propeller actually serves. It is not to move the airplane through the sky but rather serves as a large fan to keep the pilot cool. When the fan stops moving the pilot begins to sweat.

I once had an English teacher who said, "silence is golden. Let us be rich."

This was not wealth I heard.

A small airplane with a working motor is ear-damaging loud. For the longest time pilots imagined themselves as macho men and flew without headsets. The price most of us paid was irreparable damage in the years to come. An engine not making noise is a frightening thing to behold.

When a piston engine airplane runs out of fuel, the engine does not seize up and freeze the propeller. Due to the wind flowing over the nose, it keeps turning over (windmilling) at idle speed. This was the sort of lie I was now living, a worthless spinning thing up front, promising salvation but failing to deliver.

I grabbed the microphone and squeezed it in a death grip.

"One-Nine-Six-Eight Zulu declaring-in-flight-emergency" I spit out in a machine gun cadence.

In a calm voice the controller asked what aircraft had called the emergency. I was too focused to respond immediately and concentrated on the first rule in any aircraft emergency: **Fly The Airplane.** More accidents have been caused by pilots getting overwhelmed in emergency situations and forgetting the first rule.

I eventually responded. "Six-Eight Zulu with the in-flight emergency."

"Roger Six-eight Zulu. What is the nature of your emergency?"

I told them the engine had failed.

"Copy Six-eight Zulu. Will you be able to make the runway?"

"Six-eight Zulu, let me calculate" I said. What I meant was that I was praying for a divine wind.

As I looked over the city spread out beneath my wings, nothing was screaming 'land here.' I looked down at the skinny river and contemplated the odds of making a successful water landing.[38]

Thanks to my instructor, we had practiced a 'dead stick' landing some weeks earlier; bringing the airplane in with no power, the propeller stopped, and then landing on a grass strip. This off-the-book training probably did more to keep me calm than anything else.

---

[38]   A really, really bad idea, almost universally resulting in the airplane breaking up and flipping over. Only Captain Sully managed to pull off this feat on the Hudson in 2009.

"Six-eight Zulu," I responded. "I'll be able to make one-nine-left."
It was unnaturally quiet as I kept the airspeed at 70 miles per hour and began a gliding descent into the airport runway.

The Tower had diverted all incoming traffic to allow for my unimpeded arrival.

"Six-eight Zulu," he asked, *"will you need the crash truck?"*

"Negative," I replied.

I made a perfect landing, sailing over the numbers on the approach end of the runway. I had enough momentum to turn off at the first taxi way and coast to a stop.

As I looked up, there was the airport's gigantic fire and rescue truck with remote-mounted snorkel atop the cab pointed in my direction.

I hopped out of the airplane about the same time as the driver disembarked. He walked towards me in his silver asbestos suit before removing his hooded face shield. I still remember the image; the blackest face I have ever seen contrasted against the silver.

I reached into my pocket and pulled out a cigarette to calm my nerves. I could not stop my hands from shaking enough to light the cigarette.

Mister Silver-and-black looked me up and down before turning his gaze to the airplane.

"Son, that was a damn-fine landing," he said, "but if I was you, I wouldn't smoke around the airplane. It may blow up."

What I wanted to say was, *'Blow up, hell? There's no fuel.'*

What I actually said was, "You may be right," as I stuffed the cigarette back in its pack.

My flight instructor was also my boss at the massive factory. His name and contact number were on my flight plan. Upon landing, he was invited to the control tower to explain how such an inept instructor could have trained such an inept student to fly in such a reckless manner. Yikes.

The next morning, we both showed up to work, I with hat in hand and he with a FAA chastisement on his record. I was hoping to god the incident would never get farther than the two of us.

From the overhead PA system, with 50 mechanics listening – half of whom were pilots – came the following announcement: "Would '*FLAME OUT [REAL NAME REDACTED]*' please report to the line shack?"

I walked down the middle of the hangar, shaking my head in disbelief and keeping my eyes on the floor.

The mechanics stopped what they were doing, moved away from their work and, facing me, formed a sort of loose gauntlet. To a man, they erupted in thunderous laughter and applause as I made my way to the office.

In the following days many pilots came up to me, relating their own stories of bone-headed behavior and congratulating me for remembering Rule Number One and bringing the plane home safely.

My final vindication came a month later when an experimental flight crew declared an in-flight emergency and landed their business jet on a local highway. Law enforcement and the media showed up for the circus, and my boss received a call.

"Can you bring the fuel truck out?" the pilot asked sheepishly. We told him our truck was not tagged for highway use but found another truck to deliver fuel to the blocked-off roadway.

When the cute reporter thrust a microphone in the pilot's face and asked him what caused the incident, he stood a little taller, straightened his shoulders and faced the camera.

"Ma'am," the square-jawed aviator said, "these are experimental aircraft with a number of complex systems being tested and certified. We had a minor problem during a fuel transfer test and elected – for the safety of the crew and the aircraft – to make a precautionary landing."

Satisfied with the answer, the reporter cut back to the main studio.

It was in fact a fuel transfer problem; the pilots had failed to transfer fuel from our truck to their airplane prior to takeoff. I felt like a younger son in the company of my peers. Perhaps I too could become an experimental test pilot[39] someday.

———————

Other than the fuel transfer problem, my training progressed in a rapid and unimpeded manner. In December of that year, I took my check ride with an FAA Examiner, endured two hours of oral grilling, and was granted my license. As they say when they hand you the certificate, "this is really a license to learn."

Within one month of receiving my license, an unexpected promotion came my way. This pay raise allowed me to pay off flight bills and think about the future.

———————

[39]   The aircraft company I worked for employed three types of pilots. First up were the suit-and-tie Demo pilots. They were responsible for traveling with our salesmen and demonstrating new aircraft to potential buyers. To my way of thinking, this was the most polished group; able to both demonstrate the technical features of the airplane and to convince nervous buyers that it was a smart investment. Next up were the brown-jumpsuit Production Test Pilots. This group was responsible for testing certified aircraft on the production line and ensuring each airplane met all its performance criteria.   Finally there were the blue-jumpsuit Engineering Experimental Flight Test Pilots. These aviators flew our new prototype models during the initial FAA certification process, and for the most part were unflappable, chill and humble.

The exception was a younger pilot flying one of our single engine turbine-powered aircraft. He would come into the Technical Publications department, delivering performance data that we would incorporate into the flight manual. He had an insufferable manner about him that I thought needed some reorientation.

"Excuse me," I said as he walked by my desk one day, "can you empty my trash can?" "What???" he said stopping in mid-stride. "Who do you think I am?" he asked, jabbing his right index finger at a patch on his left shoulder. "I am ENGINEERING EXPERIMENTAL FLIGHT TEST."

"Oh, my bad," I said without much conviction, "I saw a blue jumpsuit. I thought you were the janitor."

Rather than starting a retirement fund, I shoveled my newfound wealth into flying faster and more-complex aircraft. Flying reminded me of skydiving in that you never reach perfection. You try to improve your skills with each flight, thinking about what you could do better next time.

I was still making skydives but could now fly an airplane to the DZ. The only question my skydiving friends ever asked was "can I jump out of it?"

We were able to accomplish this only once, realizing that it was very difficult to open a front-hinged passenger door in flight. No wonder all the skydiving planes had either moved the hinge to the top of the door sill or removed the door altogether.

At my night job I got an additional promotion. I graduated from towing small airplanes to running the fuel desk. Sometimes I would look out the window and become mesmerized by the multicolored lights adorning the taxi and runways, shimmering in the summer heat.

Row after row of all those beautiful new airplanes, sitting on the ramp, all dressed up with nowhere to go. A thought kept circulating through my head.

'They need a friend.'

A Deeply Flawed Logic

As a pilot and technically minded guy, there are certain words in the English language that I attach a very hard and unambiguous meaning to. Words like stall speed or horsepower or torque limits are, in my mind, immutable laws of God.

There is no wiggle room when the book says that you rotate the nose of a certain business jet at 104 miles per hour if the outside temperature is 98°F, the takeoff length is 5,164 feet and the atmospheric pressure is 1002 millibars. This is Moses-come-down-from-the-mountain-stuff and not open to interpretation.

In fact, each airplane has its own set of immutable God-laws called "V speeds" (velocity speeds) that are published up front in the AFM (Airplane Flight Manual). They might look something like this:

V_1 = Decision speed during takeoff to either keep going or mash the brakes and abort a takeoff
V_2 = Liftoff (or rotation) speed
V_{LE} = Maximum speed at which you extend the landing gear
V_{NE} = The never-exceed speed for the airplane (it's maximum safe operating speed)
V_S = The speed at which your machine will fall out of the sky (stall speed) and give you an opportunity to explain to God why you broke his law

It can be an exhaustive list, yet pilots are expected to memorize these very precise data points.

So, on one hand I swear allegiance to the purity of definitions.

But due to circumstances of my own making, there is another set of words in which I offer a wider latitude of interpretation. Words like *Grand Theft* and *Federal Crimes* seem a little heavy-handed. I would prefer the term *'borrowed.'*

Likewise, the judgmental term *'Drug pilot'* might be more gently expressed as *'independent contract pilot services.'*

Taking such liberties with the English language, I might be able to explain how I borrowed an airplane from the FBO, flew it thousands of miles to the Caribbean, and used it for contract pilot services without painting myself into a disreputable corner.

It started, as all bad ideas do, with self-delusion and a sort of moral relativism.

———————

The late 1970s and into the early 1980s were both the halcyon days and the end-of-days for small airplane manufacturing companies. Cessna and Beechcraft, the industry giants out of Wichita, were cranking out a bewildering number of small aircraft. A host of other smaller manufacturers scattered throughout the country were also doing their best to spit out aircraft in record numbers.

Cessna was considered the Chevy of the marketplace while Beech had positioned its smaller product offerings as the Cadillac version of Detroit.

Founded in 1927, Cessna was the king of iterative design. Their signature look was a high-wing, single-engine plane with tricycle landing gear. It took a keen eye and ear to separate the various models as they flew overhead in ever-increasing numbers.

The only problem was that nobody was buying. At a time before the Federal Reserve began cooking their books and under-reporting data, interest rates in 1980 were approaching 18%. This was killing consumer demand on almost all items, let alone the luxury purchases of private aircraft.

Wichita plane manufacturers, and Cessna in particular, were adding to the problem by forcing dealers to accept new airplanes they could not sell. The inevitable result was that new and unsold inventory was stacking up across the Midwest like cord wood.

You couldn't fly into an airport without seeing row after row after row of shiny new aircraft, all waiting in vain for a buyer. And of all the aircraft manufacturers with their myriad of offerings, none were as plentiful and ubiquitous as the Cessna 172, a four-seater capable of flying 500 miles over a four-hour period.

They were everywhere, sitting in the sun, slowly deteriorating, and from our perspective at the FBO, just begging to be exercised.

Many of us working the night shift were pilots and one night a sort of mass hypnosis fell over us all as we waited for the occasional customer.

"It's kind of a shame that those airplanes are just sitting out there, wasting away," said Ralph.

"Yeah," added one of the newer pilots who had wandered in one night and become a regular on-site loafer. "I read that the worst thing you can do to an airplane is just let it set. The seals get hard, the tires develop flat spots, and the cable pulleys take a hard set."

A consensus began to build as we looked at the lock box on the wall, containing almost 65 sets of keys to new aircraft.

"Hum," I offered. "It might not be a bad thing to start them from time to time just to get the engine oil lubricating."

The idea took off like wildfire, and it wasn't too many days before we made the leap in our minds from running up the engines to taking airplanes around the patch. We didn't exactly see this as theft as much as helping Cessna keep their inventory in tip-top shape.

What's in a name anyway? One man's idea of grand theft larceny is just another man's idea of a joy ride. And if you put it back when you are done, who's to know the difference? Shouldn't we be charging Cessna for helping to preserve their assets while in our care and custody?

This was the sort of deeply flawed logic that began to float around in our heads. It allowed us a sort of sloppy mental justification to begin taking various airplanes out on semi-nightly joy rides. Once we even left the state and did a few touch-and-goes to stay current.

And just as one thing leads to another, Vince was about to reappear in my life and offer me some easy money.

I Get the Call

I had been working the weekend shift, and for once was able to leave at 5 pm. I headed down the street to our crew's unofficial hangout. *'Walter's Cum-n-Go Liquor,'* the sign said, and at the time it was legal to drink in their parking lot.

The store was located just off the airport, and airplanes would pass directly overhead while coming in for a landing. We would prop ourselves up on a car hood, lean back against the windshield, pass a joint between us and drink cheap Pabst Blue Ribbon as plane after plane made its final approach.

I must say we were stone cold stupid at the time, and it's worth noting that the country itself had fallen into what I came to think of as *The Stupor of the Times*.

It was the era of Jimmy Carter in office, and of the most forgettable and horrible car designs to ever come out of Detroit. It was an era of high inflation with no one at the helm. It was a post-Watergate and post-Vietnam world where America had lost its rudder.

It was a free for all in Miami with drugs and money flooding into town, putting ill-gotten gains into a building frenzy unequaled since.

It was an era inside the assembly plant where airplanes kept failing their oxygen system checks because workers were stealing little aluminum fittings and smoking pot out of them.

It was an era when NASA employees regularly drank their lunch and returned to work, approving O-ring designs for the space shuttle program.

It was in this time of general malaise that I looked out across the ramp one afternoon and saw my coworkers, having just returned from a pot-infused lunch, chattering away happily on top of our fuel truck, striking matches and lighting their cigarettes.

As the beer disappeared and the sun began to set, I offered my observations to the crew.

"Really, for fuck's sake," I said, "what were you doing smoking on top of the fuel truck?"

Gibbel, an Arkansas transplant who was missing front teeth after a lead-pipe encounter in the distant past, offered his own understanding of chemistry and physics. "It's got a tank cover. The lid was closed. I checked it myself."

"It's not the fuel that ignites," I said in exasperation. "It's the fumes that come out of the escape valve. The one you guys were sitting on."

"Oh," he said as if processing some deep truth. "Okay."

———————

I headed out from the parking lot back to my tiny house. The roof still sagged, the neighbors were still obnoxious, and the pathetic window unit was still trying to keep up. The answering machine was blinking.

"Hey, it's Vince," said the voice on the recorder. "I got a deal for you. Please call me back as soon as you can. Thanks."

Since first meeting at the university four years earlier, we had stayed in touch. He had been climbing the drug distribution ladder and proved to have a natural skill at putting buyers and sellers together in ever-increasing amounts.

He had apparently outgrown his Chicago connection and was now dealing with folks out of the Florida Keys. Like all organizations, there was an amount of internal friction and competition among the distributors. At the time it was just a low simmer. In months to come it would turn into an all-consuming forest fire.

I dialed his number and reached him on the third ring.

"This isn't something we can discuss on the phone," he said, "but can I come see you tomorrow?"

I gave him my address and told him we could meet over lunch. I was guessing Vince wanted to expand his distribution network and was looking for a local connection. Like branching out in Amway. That wasn't me.

I never enjoyed that part of the business, and was always worried when my dealer friends were forced to interact with unknown buyers.

———————

Vince showed up the next day at the restaurant. Thin, short, wiry with a neatly groomed mustache, he was a ball of energy and had an instantly likable personality to match.

He was the kind of guy a girl might take home to mother, and mom would invite him to stay for supper. With a warm handshake and an affable spirit, you just naturally wanted to buy whatever Vince was selling.

"I've got a proposition for you," he began.

"Not interested Vince," I interrupted. 'I don't want to be a distributor."

"No, not what I'm talking about," he continued. "I remember you got your pilot license a while back. What can you fly?"

"What do you mean, what can I fly?"

"How big?" he continued. "Like how much can it hold?"

"Up to six people, including me."

"Not what I'm asking. How much weight can it haul?"

"Depends on the aircraft Vince," I said evenly. "Why?"

"Well, here's the deal. I got some guys in Miami that need a pilot."

"For what?"

"Well," and he hesitated, "they need to get a shipment out of Jamaica."

"You are shitting me. Really?"

"For real," he continued. "One time deal, …. or maybe more. Depends."

"Don't they have a pilot?"

"Well," and he hesitated a bit longer, "they did, but he[40] ran into some trouble. He crash-landed off the coast of Cuba and their Navy rescued him. Took him to jail. Looks like he will there for a while."

"Sorry Vince," I finished, "I've got no interest in that. But just for curiosity, what's it pay?"

"$20,000," he said without missing a beat.

Humm, enough money to buy a used airplane, get that Bang & Olufsen system I always wanted, move into a nice apartment …….. The stupor of the times was in full effect.

Money is a powerful intoxicant, and Archimedes said that with a long enough lever and fulcrum you could move the earth. Apparently, it was not taking a very big lever to move my world. I leaned into his pitch and listened hard.

"Here's the thing," he said, "we'll fly down to Miami and meet these guys. No pressure, no commitment. It's just a meet and greet. See what you think. If they like you and you're comfortable with them, we go from there."

"What could it hurt?" I responded, and he closed the deal.

---

[40] A high school typing teacher out of Key West. At the time, everybody was moving pot out of the Caribbean by any and all means possible. The mayor of Key West was reliably reported to be moving cocaine. Bill Clinton had a thing going on in Mena, Arkansas and Vice President George H.W. Bush was knee-deep into kickbacks, overseeing the South Florida Drug Task Force out of Miami.

A Heat Like No Other

Stepping out of the Miami airport and into the South Florida heat was like entering a sauna. My glasses fogged up immediately, and I began to perspire. Even though the real terror of summer had not shown its face, it was remarkably uncomfortable for a Midwest boy.

The black Audi rolled curbside; its window tint almost as dark as the paint. It looked sinister, and as the driver rolled down the passenger window, I was struck with a thought that its occupants gave off the same ominous vibe.

"Vince," said Johnny leaning across the steering wheel, "you and your buddy get in."

Johnny was lean and sinewy with a chiseled jawline, dark glasses to match and dressed in black to boot. He had a Latin bloodline look about him, but I never knew his last name.

Sitting next to him was his cousin Alex, heavy set with dark eyes that were constantly darting back and forth, like he was expecting trouble at any second. Instinctively, I thought, *'this is a guy who could not be trusted.'*

We pulled out of the airport and made small chitchat while Johnny blasted down I-95 at high speed, weaving in and out of traffic like some kind of Indy 500 driver. He honked the horn, flashed his lights, showed impatience with drivers who would not get out of his way,[41] and all the while displaying a hyper alert neurosis.

We passed Miami and kept heading south towards Homestead and the Card Sound Road cutoff. As we entered The Keys proper at North Key Largo, I caught my first glimpse of that famous stretch of highway leading southwest across the open waters of the Florida Keys.

---

[41] Even today when driving down I-95 and watching fast sedans with blacked-out windows weave in and out of traffic I can't help but think it's another self-important South Florida drug dealer on his way to The Keys.

It took my breath away, and from the backseat I soaked in a flood of images; boats in the water, outcroppings of mobile homes next to million-dollar houses, fishing and tackle stores everywhere, Florida skinnies with long beards who looked like central casting extras from Robinson Crusoe and everywhere the spectacular blue water.

The sun was setting as we pulled into Johnny's waterfront house in Marathon. It was multi-story with south facing access to the water and was easily 6,000 square feet. He came to a quick stop at the gate and simultaneously punched in a code while triggering the garage door. Within ten seconds we were gliding into the multi-car garage and the heavy gate was closing behind us.

It was a quick and stealthy movement, as if he did not want to appear in public for any length of time.

Johnny volunteered nothing about himself, but I learned from Vince that his day job was working for the IRS.

Perfect. Who would know better than an agent how to hide assets from an agent?

We entered the house from the garage level. Chrome and glass stairs led to the main level, and the entire floor was covered with floor-to-ceiling glass. The exterior shutters were all rolled down, making the interior feel like an impenetrable fortress.

"What's your name, and what's your experience?" he asked, handing me a Red Stripe.

"Bill Mahoney," I said.

In this business nobody was giving out particulars.

"As for flying, I've got about 200 hours flying single-engine planes. Complex, retract, high performance. But nothing in this line of work."

"We lost our pilot a few weeks ago," he continued. "We need something that will haul 300 pounds. Six bales[42] at 50 pounds each. Prearranged drop to a boat sitting just off Marathon.

"Standard flight plan coming out of Jamaica, back over Cuba and then a straight shot back to Marathon. When you start your descent, the boat will signal you. You kick the bales out while on descent and we pick them up. When you land, you're good."

"Flying over Cuba," I asked with surprise. "How?"

"Done all the time," said Johnny. "Special GIRON corridor that Cuba has set up for non-commercial flights between here and Jamaica. You just need to file for clearance beforehand. We've got a WAC chart[43] around here somewhere"

Johnny knew a tremendous amount about the intricacies of the route and had served as a kicker many times, throwing bales out of the airplane to waiting boats below.

"Alex will fly out with you to Jamaica, make all the arrangements and show you the landing field. Once the aircraft gets loaded, you will fly back with Vince as your kicker. Oh, and you supply the plane."

"I've got something in mind," I said thinking about the lonesome airplanes sitting back at the FBO. "A Cessna. It will handle the load, but how long is the strip I would be landing at?"

---

[42] Sometimes bales would get lost in the nighttime seas. The next morning, they would wash in with the tide to Miami-area beaches. These errant bales were known in South Florida as 'square groupers.' You might get greedy and try to cash in on your good fortune, but who do you know that wants to buy 50 pounds of pot at a time?

[43] World Aeronautical Chart. A pilot's map showing relevant radio frequencies, navigational aids and other information overlaid on a topographical view of Cuba and Jamaica.

"I don't know, but it's massive," he said. "Been in and out with a couple of large twins, so you shouldn't have any problems."

"Twenty grand?" I asked.

"Vince?" asked Johnny as he looked over my shoulder.

"Yeah, that's on me," replied Vince.

I had a few thoughts running around my head. One was that I had enough faith in Vince to know the money was for real. A second thought was that Johnny was a deadly-serious guy and not to be crossed. A third thought was that $20,000 was a nice amount of folding money in my pocket. A fourth thought was that with a borrowed airplane my overhead cost would be quite low.

A final thought was that this looked like a cakewalk. The Sirens were singing loudly, pulling me in deeply toward the shoals.

"Yes," I affirmed with full resolve and yet very little real understanding.

"We got things to arrange on our end," Johnny said. "Can you be back in a week?"

"Shouldn't be a problem. I'll stay in touch with Vince and let him know if there is a delay, but I can be back here next Friday."

Johnny looked me hard in the eyes. "Alright," he said. "You're in."

What I heard in my mind was that I had just made a deal with the devil. If I messed up or failed to deliver there would be hell to pay.

Alex listened but said very little.

Johnny ordered pizza, and we spent the night discussing specific details of the flight. Vince and Alex got high, but Johnny and I abstained. We were on a more professional footing - if there is such a thing among thieves.

As the evening concluded, Vince and I were shown into the guest quarters, offering a spectacular view of the waterfront through sliding glass doors that led out to a wrap-around balcony.

It was a sort of dreamscape, and I thanked Vince for letting me into the big leagues.

––––––––––––

The next day Alex drove us back to the airport in his Alfa GTV, a cramped but stylish ride.

Johnny had a day job to attend to; auditing tax files on behalf of the United States government for those sneaks and cheats who were under-reporting income.

Something Borrowed, Something Blue

I walked into the FBO and said hello to my counterpart behind the desk. He was also a pilot and had been helping to keep the forgotten Cessnas in tip top condition.

"Shane, I need to borrow an airplane for a few days," I said lying. "I need to get current and do a little cross country."

"You've nuts, you know that right? This shit's gotta stop. One of these days somebody is going to notice these missing planes. I don't want any part of this," he concluded, "but you know where the keys are."

I headed over to the lock box, stuffed full of keys with round paper tags identifying the airplane by N number. I picked out an airplane that I had flown before, cream colored base coat with a beautiful blue trim job.

"I'll bring it back in two days," I said heading out the door and down the ramp.

That night I flew the 172 to my hometown airport and prepared for a long, long, long cross country. I would be flying by visual flight rules, using all the skills I had developed to plot out courses, track VOR[44]s, avoid weather systems and land time and again to refuel.

The next morning before departing, I got a really stupid – or inspired – idea and changed the registration number displayed on the airplane. My thinking was that if the Feds found out a plane had been borrowed and looked into their system, at least the factory-assigned N number would not show up.

---

[44] Variable Omni-directional Range. A radio navigation system linked between the airplane and strategically placed ground stations. These stations, when coupled with special instruments in the cockpit, allow a pilot to create an invisible tracking line in the sky.

I purchased the registration numbers from a mechanic friend, peeled off the existing registration as he watched and placed the new numbers on the sides of the fuselage. What he thought of my activity remained locked inside his head.

My plan was for a five-day trip. Two days down, one day in Jamaica and two days back to the Midwest. Maybe not the two days I had promised Shane but close enough in my mind.

———————————

The trip to The Keys was without incident. It was good weather across the Southeast, and I was helped by an occasional tailwind. Being very mindful of fuel management, I made stops every four hours and arrived in Marathon after 10 hours of flight time.

Vince and Alex picked me up at the airport. We packed the plane for an early departure and headed back to Johnny's for a night's sleep.

The next morning, I called the FAA with a flight plan and requested clearance to fly the GIRON corridor over Cuba. Clearance was granted but with a one day wait requirement. We unpacked the airplane and spent the night at a local bar eating raw oysters and drinking more Red Stripe beer.

We departed early the next morning and headed southeast over the open water, flying on a compass heading of 135° and threading our way between an unseen land mass on our left (the Bahamas) and an unseen land mass on our right (Cuba).

At some exact point in this open water, we would make a hard right turn, fly for another 40 minutes and eventually spot Cuba. If my calculations were correct, we would fly over the island unchallenged. If my piloting was flawed and I missed the corridor, we could be shot down.

Ancient philosophers spoke about a silver cord, invisible to the eye that connects flesh with spirit. When the silver cord is severed, death occurs. Or maybe it's the other way around; after death the silver cord is broken. For pilots, this silver cord is a faint radio signal emitted from the VOR and picked up by the airplane's navigational radios.

Flying across the vast and featureless water, there is nothing visual to help answer the two fundamental questions of 'where are we' and 'are we on track?' It's much easier when flying over land. You look down and see a railroad track crossing a highway with a factory nearby. The map shows all of these items, confirming your position and giving you a sense of relief.

None of these visual cues exist over water. It's just mile after mile of beautiful aqua-marine water.

You start out with a map, a pencil and a special ruler drawing lines to your destination. It's a simple math exercise, so many miles per hour and an airplane that goes so fast. In four hours and six minutes you will be there.

But nature conspires in so many ways against you. The compass is a liar, because hidden lines of magnetic flux weave their spell under the earth and influence the reading. The map says to fly a precise heading of 135° but to do so you must compensate for the magnetic influence and fly a compass heading of 142°.

The wind forecast said that you can expect a 12 mile per hour breeze coming out the south. In order to keep your true course of 142° you must point the nose a little more into the wind. But if the wind is stronger, weaker or out of another direction, it will blow you off course.

You fly in a sort of blind faith, and the thin silver cord of the VOR is your ultimate truth. It's projecting an invisible straight line across the earth and your only real job is to maneuver the airplane in such a manner that it keeps flying right above it. Yet the cord weakens over distance and becomes quieter, less reliable and fainter. In time it goes silent.

Then you are alone, looking at the water, trying to perceive if you are drifting one way or another. The compass tells you all is well, but you know it is an unreliable witness.

You twist another knob, find a new VOR and connect to its silver cord. It confirms your location and lets you know the ship has been pushed off to the north by the invisible hand. It's time to press harder on the right rudder and nose the ship a little more toward the south.

Amelia Earhart and her navigator must have felt this sense of dread when they flew aimlessly through the Pacific air, looking for an impossibly small dot in the ocean. Hoping without reason to find a silver cord that would connect them back to the earth, and failing such, to fly until every last ounce of fuel had been consumed and they glided silently to their deaths.

The worst has not yet been mentioned. If you are a VFR pilot, you have been taught to fly using your eyes. They are reliable instruments until the clouds close in, and then all hell can break lose. When you lose your visual reference and start looking around the cockpit, you can induce a deadly thing known as vertigo.

You will swear that your airplane has flipped upside down, but it hasn't. Your ears are lying and singing a death song to you. If you believe your senses and try to fly by feel, you will make obscenely wrong inputs to the control surfaces. Inevitably, these wrong responses will cause the airplane to flip into a crazy and unrecoverable attitude.

The airplane will respond to your wrong thinking and scream towards the earth. Sometimes the force is so great it rips the wings from the fuselage. And then it ends suddenly. The FAA will record the cause of death as 'impact.'

Accident investigators think this is what happened to John F. Kennedy, Jr. when he crashed his small plane off the coast of Martha's Vineyard in late 1999.

An old WWII pilot friend told me his stories once; of being shot at without having defensive guns, at flying straight and level over the Himalayas and suddenly feeling a great hand of violent air driving them down toward the mountain peaks, unable to escape its grasp. But the hardest thing of all, he said, was believing his instruments and keeping the plane level when his physical senses were screaming exactly the opposite.[45]

As we flew along the silver cord, I imagined one last gremlin. Although the airplane was brand new, from time to time I would swear the engine missed a beat. So did my heart.

---

[45] Though not instrument rated at the time, I experienced this more than once when getting caught in the clouds. I would have sworn that my legs were over my head and that the plane was completely upside down and sideways. But I looked at my instruments and saw the airplane was flying straight and level.

But we remained true to our course and after two hours of flying in a certain direction I headed south for the unseen land of Cuba. As we got closer, I began communications with their air traffic controllers and picked up the navigation aid for the GIRON corridor. We spotted land and flew precisely over the corridor. In twenty minutes, Cuba was behind us. Our next stop was Montego Bay.

I thought of Johnny's pilot who had not successfully navigated the trip. He was now sitting in a Cuban jail without much hope of immediate release. His failure resulted in the loss of 3 square groupers and had also forced the Monroe County school district to find a long-term sub for their now-missing typing teacher.

Had I known in advance their pilot was a middle school instructor, it might have given me pause to reflect on the professional caliber of the whole organization. But to quote lyrics from Minx, a Midwest music group, "Baby, I'm all in."

As we approached the northwest corner of Jamaica, I began communicating with Montego Bay air traffic controllers. We were vectored in for a landing and made a gentle approach with controllers guiding both my altitude and heading at the largely commercial airport.

It was a smooth landing, and ground control instructed us to taxi to the customs ramp. I performed my shut down checklist and secured the control surfaces as a kindred soul from their local FBO tied down our plane.

We met with Customs and were herded into their building. It was mind bending for me to hear perfect King's English coming from the black-skinned Jamaican official. Some years later I would begin to study the Caribbean in earnest, understanding the European colonization efforts that abused and overlaid virtually every island in the region.

He informed me that the flight plan I filed was designated for flight crew only and wanted to know who the two passengers were. "Copilot," I said pointing to Vince and "navigator" looking over at Alex.

With a nod that implied a sense of suspended disbelief, he stamped the documents and let us pass into the terminal area.

As we stepped out into the taxi stand a beat-up Toyota Corona wheeled to the curb.

"Get in mahn," the voice said in a cadence I associated with Bob Marley and the Wailers. It was Nelson, an associate of Johnny and Alex.

"Ah saw you comin' in and landin' in dat bluejay," he said. "Nice plane. You gonna take it into da mountains?" he asked me as he pointed off to the east.

"That's the plan," I said.

"Brave lad," he said displaying a mouth full of white teeth. "You fly'n long?"

"A couple of years," I responded.

"Brave lad," he finished evenly. "You got you some balls mahn."

Nelson sped out of the airport parking lot, driving on the left side of the road. It was my first experience with the British traffic system, and I was never able to fully reprogram my mind to look for oncoming traffic in what appeared to be the wrong direction.

He dropped Vince and I off at the nearest airport hotel while Alex stayed in the car.

"I've got some business to attend to," Alex said from the passenger side window. "We'll come by around ten tomorrow morning. Get some rest."

We checked into the hotel and took the only room available near the back entrance. I was grateful that English was our common language, and after a few hours I began to successfully decipher that colorful Jamaican dialect with its playful sing-song rhythm.

After unpacking we headed down the street to scout out supper. Local vendors were on every corner grilling up fish, jerk[46]and chicken.

---

[46]   A traditional pork dish created with a blended variety of spices. Often over-cooked to a consistency of beef jerky.

We picked up a plate of chicken, located a six pack of Red Stripe and made our way back to the hotel. I was exhausted from the day's flight and barely made it through two beers and half a plate of chicken before turning in. Vince stayed up late watching shadowy images on the black and white tele.

About three in the morning, I woke up to use the bathroom. I glanced over at my unfinished supper and saw a black blob covering it. Turning on the light, I realized it was thousands upon thousands of ants intent on dissembling the chicken into tiny pieces.

The line snaked away from the plate, up the cracked lime green wall and over the windowsill. It must have been a quarter-inch wide and ten feet long. I watched in fascination as this disciplined army moved my chicken up and out of the bathroom.

The next morning, I examined the plate. The chicken had been fully stripped to the bone with no sign of the previous night's activity. I told the desk clerk that ants had invaded my room. I wanted to know what they could do about it.

"You leave some food out sir?" he asked.

"Yes, I did."

"Donn' leave da food out," he suggested. "Dem ants wonn' come round no more."

Chastised and so informed, I went down to the pool and ordered coffee and a light breakfast. The hotel was strategically positioned on a hill overlooking the airport. I scanned the tarmac and saw my 172 tied down in the distance. All looked well.

The only other guest was a blond-haired guy about my age and with a build that resembled Vince's. He was wearing mirrored sunglasses and appeared to be looking in my direction. I gave him a universal head nod and he returned the same.

A double shot of espresso arrived, and I lit up a Dunhill. Coffee and cigarettes were such an integrated pair that I never considered one without the other.

As I took a drag off my cigarette, the singular guest strolled casually over to my table.

"Mind if I sit down?" he asked.

"Be my guest," I responded and pointed to an open seat.

"I noticed you flew in yesterday afternoon in Nine-Alpha-Quebec," he said rattling off my N number with apparent nonchalance.

"Yes," I said trying to hide my surprise.

"First time here?"

"Yep."

"What brings you to this lovely spot?"

"Got a couple of buddies that want to do some scuba diving. I flew them over from The Keys."

This guy apparently read me like a book from front to back in twenty seconds without flinching.

"Uh huh," he responded, obviously not believing my story. "What's your name?"

"Bill Mahoney," I said.

He rocked back in his chair and removed his sunglasses, displaying piercing and startlingly blue eyes.

"What did you say?" he asked, tilting his head, as if to lean into my answer.

"Bill Mahoney."

"You have got to be kidding me," he finally said with a laugh and huge grin. "My best friend back in Jersey goes by the name of William Mahoney. That's unbelievable. I'm Jimmy," he said extending his hand. "Nice to meet you, Bill."

I didn't give him my real name but told him a short version of how I came to adopt Bill Mahoney. I wasn't sure if he was really 'Jimmy', but we had established a cover identity that suited both of us. He told me about his "associate" back in Jersey, and we both laughed at the implausibility of shared names.

"Look," he said laying down his cards. "I live here in the hotel. I watch everything that comes in and out of the airport. You didn't arrive with any scuba gear. I know what you are here for."

"What's that?" I responded.

"You are going to pick up a load somewhere east of here and fly it out. Based on your airplane I'd say about 250 pounds worth. Not a huge load but respectable. And I would guess you'll drop it off back in The Keys."

I was truly stunned. Had somebody stenciled the words 'drug pilot' in infrared ink over my forehead? Was this like the movie *They Live* in which the lead character found a pair of special sunglasses that revealed aliens walking around New York City and hidden messages in the billboards?

I held my hands up in a sort of mock surrender gesture.

"It's fine," he continued. "I've got my own operation here. What you do is your business. I won't interfere. What I really wanted to know is if you are available this weekend to fly over to the Bahamas. I'm down a pilot and need to get a small load moved to Ft. Lauderdale. It's worth $10,000."

Wow, wow, wow. I had stumbled headlong into what looked like never-ending opportunities flying in the Caribbean as a free-lance pilot. Incredible. Was everybody over here in the business?

"Thanks for the offer, Jimmy," I said with real sincerity, "but I'm committed to these guys, and we hope to be off this weekend."

"No worries, Bill," he finished. "Let me know if your schedule frees up. If I'm not here, the front desk knows where to find me. Just ask for Jimmy."

He got up to leave and I arose from the table as well. I shook his hand, and he drew me in for a surprisingly warm embrace.

"Fucking Bill Mahoney," he said again laughing. "Unbelievable. I gotta call my buddy today and tell him I met his younger brother."

He walked away, shaking his head and chuckling to himself. Vince rounded the corner and headed in my direction.

"Who was that?" he asked as he sat down.

"You wouldn't believe me if I told you," I said, "but it looks like we may not be alone in this business here on the island."

Alex and Nelson showed up two hours late, around noon. As we got in the car Alex announced there had been a change of schedule. We were driving over to Kingston to meet somebody named Russ. As I knew none of the players or the back-end logistics of this deal, nothing seemed amiss to me.

We took the A1 ring road that encircles Jamaica, hugging the northern coast with occasional views of the ocean on the left and, somewhere off to my right, the yet-to-be surveyed landing strip.

Although the topography southeast of Montego Bay didn't meet my definition of a mountain range, the 1,500-foot peaks and valleys were steep, technically challenging and looked ominous.

Continuing eastward for another 40 minutes, we headed south at Ocho Rios and wheeled into town around 3 p.m. To my eye, Kingston appeared to be grimier and rougher than Montego Bay.

It may be that the pirating history of the area, stretching back into the 17th century when every fourth building was said to be a brothel or a tavern, had left a permanent mark on the capital city and nearby Port Royal.

The business end of these deals remained a mystery to me throughout the trip. If you take a street value of $1,000 per pound, and I delivered 300 pounds, that's roughly $300,000. Maybe Johnny bought this load for half the amount. But where did that money come from in the first place?

Was it like Target lay-away or ninety-days-same-as-cash? Did Johnny wire the money through Western Union or write the Jamaicans a check? Did these guys take American Express?

If it was a cash business – and I knew it was - how did that much money make it from The Keys back to Montego Bay?

In watching the streaming series *Narcos,* you might get an idea of the vast amount of corruption involved at every level during this time. Whole countries like Panama were involved.

Banks as big as HSBC may have been knee-deep in corrupted dollars, and Miami's commercial building development was at least partially fueled by ill-gotten gains. We are talking billions of dollars at a time when a million was a large sum.

Johnny's operations might have been a drop in the bucket to most of the big players. It might have been why Jimmy didn't care what I was doing in-country. But to Johnny it was his revenue stream, and I suspect he was always 30 days late with the bill collectors. I was just one cog in his complex machine.

Checking into another subpar hotel, we met Russ. He would be driving the boat that Vince and I would drop to. Any fancy ideas I had about communication were soon put to rest.

"Hell no I don't have a radio to talk to you," he said. "I'll be listening to Tower as you come in. About five minutes before touchdown, I'll flash you six times with a spotlight and begin circling my boat. That's your signal. When you see me circling, start the drop."

"Will each bale have a beacon attached to it?" I asked.

"What? No. You just kick them out. I'll follow your flight path in and get them out of the water."

This plan seemed a lot looser than I had imagined. But being the rookie pilot, I didn't ask any questions.

"Where is the landing strip?" I asked Alex. "It looks like rugged terrain to the east of Montego Bay. Johnny said you'd show it to me."

"We don't have time for that," offered Alex. "I'll mark it on your map. You can't miss it."

We spent the night in Kingston, and I got in a fight with Alex over his treatment of a hooker. Drunk and boisterous, he began hurling insults and comments I thought were indefensible. Maybe it was the beer and pot convincing me a hooker's honor needed to be defended. Maybe it was the general angst building up in my head.

Whatever it was, we got into a shouting match that was headed towards blows. Nelson finally interceded, putting us both in our corner and sending the girl packing.

The next day's drive back to Montego Bay was in silence. Vince was trying to not take sides but seemed torn between our friendship and business with Johnny's associates. We were dropped off at the hotel without much comment.

Later that day Alex came over to offer both an apology and a schedule change. We were delayed four more days. No explanation was given, and I was at the mercy of someone else's timeline.

I began to think about the two-day promise I made Shane back at our FBO. We were now five days out and counting. Ten days did not seem out of the question. Shit, shit, shit.

In the days of waiting, my mind went from being chill to being fraught with anxiety. While I was concerned that the airplane would be missed, there was nothing I could do about it.

The logistics of the flight itself were also worrying. The mountain strip, the flight over Cuba, the drop, the eventual return of my plane. All of it was overwhelming, but it did no good to run hypothetical scenarios through my mind. Time would bring whatever clarity it brought.

Vince and I spent the idle days knocking around the Bay area, mingling with legitimate tourists and buying pot off the locals who roamed the beach. We got introduced to a group of Rastafarians who sold us a 'spliff' one day.

This remains the largest hand-rolled pot cigarette I had ever seen or smoked. It was so comically large that I thought it was a joke. But the Rasta insisted we smoke it all. I think I remember waking up a few hours later on the beach, having inadvertently destroyed one of my contact[47] lens.

Another afternoon I wandered over to the city dump, meeting locals and helping them pick through trash in hopes of salvaging something worth selling. Call it my Peace Corp for a day contribution to global harmony.

On day nine we got the word. The shipment was ready and whatever mysterious back-room financial machinations that were required had been fulfilled. Alex and Russ would be leaving in a few hours, getting the boat ready back in Marathon. Vince and I would be flying out the next day and picking up the load.

The routine had been laid out to me a few days earlier and was apparently working. We would file a standard flight plan out of Montego Bay and depart the airport. At around 25 miles out, the relatively weak Jamaican radar would be unable to track us further. When Departure told us that "radar service is terminated" we would dive down to the water, turn around and head back to the coast.

---

[47]   Back in the day I wore hard contact lenses. As crazy or stupid as it sounds, I would sometimes take them out before sleeping (or passing out) and place them between my upper lip and gum as a temporary storage place. This was in lieu of a contact case and solution, which never seemed to be available when I needed it. When I awoke, I would wet them with saliva and reinsert them into my eyes.

On this particular day, I dreamed I had ingested sand in my mouth and was busy spitting it out. When I returned to consciousness, I realized that I had been nibbling away on my right contact, spitting it out one tiny piece after another.

Intercepting the shoreline east of Montego Bay, we would fly nap of the earth until reaching the landing site. There we would be quickly loaded up with the bales and take off again. Skimming the water until 40 miles away from the coastline, we would climb back up to our original flight plan.

The entire diversion took about 45 minutes and was added into our flight plan time so that the FAA was none the wiser. If all went well, I would be landing around sunset, allowing Russ to see square groupers as they tumbled from the sky.

On departure morning, Vince and I left the hotel with minimal baggage (and no scuba gear). We cleared Customs easily and arrived at the airplane. After fueling up, I paid the line service worker a generous tip and we taxied out to the runway. I reflected on the audacity, stupidity, hubris and courage of this whole affair. I was 21 years old and engaged in a high risk, high reward endeavor.

I thought about those WWII pilots who were of a similar age and with similar flight time. Trained at air bases like the DZ I had lived at, they were put in control of hastily designed bombers and pointed towards Germany in thousand-plane formations. They carried the weight of the free world on their shoulders while facing a very uncertain future.

In May of 1943 the B-17 bomber *Memphis Belle* was celebrated for being the first crew to fly 25 missions without getting shot down. While no one was going to pin a medal on me for flying this route, there were similar elements of a great adventure unfolding. Philosopher Joseph Campbell might have called it a 'Hero's Journey.'

As we taxied out to our great adventure, I changed from Ground to Tower frequency. They cleared us for an immediate takeoff and confirmed our flight plan.

"Nine-Alpha-Quebec cleared for takeoff Runway Seven. Right turn zero-one-zero. Climb and maintain five thousand five hundred."

I read back the instructions and moved the throttle to the firewall. We were off the runway in 2,000 feet and I turned left to the assigned compass heading. Tower handed us over to their version of Departure Control.

We climbed quickly to 5,500 feet, leveled off and maintained our compass heading of 010°. We watched as the miles ticked by and listened as Departure Control said the magic words, *"Radar Service Terminated."*

I waited another two minutes and looked over at Vince.

"Okay brother," I said, "here we go."

Down The Rabbit Hole

Retarding the throttle to 1,700 rpms and adding carburetor heat for good measure, I banked the plane over to the right and began a quick descent, mindful of the lessons I learned about diving too rapidly and shock-cooling the engine.

According to the map, we needed to be about 25 miles east of Montego Bay before we made landfall, and I plotted this point. As I approached the coastline we appeared to be on track, but skimming the earth presented its own problems in locating the landing strip. Without altitude and the bird's eye view it provides, we could be right beside the strip and miss is in the next valley over.

"Coming up on two miles," Vince said as he scanned the terrain below looking at the map. "One mile and I don't see a thing." Another minute crept by, and we were both beginning to get nervous. Flying back from Jamaica without the load was its own death sentence. Flying into the hillside was another kind of death sentence. Getting caught by Customs was another sort of death sentence. Suddenly, the easy money part of the equation was fading into the distance.

About the time I was ready to seriously panic Vince shouted out, "there it is. At the one o'clock position. Do you see it?"

I looked at the area he was pointing out. It was a straight line running north and south, lighter in color and tucked in the middle of two steep hills. In no way did it resemble Johnny's description of 'a massive runway.'

"That?" I recoiled. "Are you sure?"

"Well, no," he said in disgust, "I'm not sure. I have never been here before. Remember? But I think that's it. It's the only thing around."

I took another look and committed to at least making a low pass. There were no flashing 'land here' lights to help with the determination.

"Alright, hold on," I said as I banked the plane hard right in an effort to put the runway on my left[48].

"You're going the wrong way," Vince shouted.

"Shut up Vince, I know what I am doing," I responded in a statement that wasn't strictly true.

Flying in these conditions, where the runway drops into a valley, I had to skim the surrounding hillsides as part of the approach to landing.

When I had lined up the runway behind my left shoulder, I brought the power back to flight idle and placed the flaps into the fully extended position. This caused the plane to pitch nose down until I adjusted the trim wheel.

"Shit, we're gonna die," Vince said as he adopted that most primal of male gestures and clutched his crotch.

"No, we're not," I said as I adjusted power and began a moderate turn back towards what I assumed was the strip. Most takeoff and landing accidents happen during this banking phase; when you need to keep your airspeed up, the bank angle shallow and the airplane flying true. I kept the airspeed pegged at 70 miles per hour and lined up to land.

I am hesitant to mention divine protection in the commission of a crime, but there was a palpable sense of deep peace as we lined up on short final.

I kept my hand on the throttle in case this was not the landing strip, but everything felt right. As I came over the far end of the runway, I moved the throttle back to idle and let the Cessna begin to bleed off airspeed.

---

[48]   In airplanes, the pilot or captain's seat is always on the left. Unless otherwise directed by Traffic Controllers or natural obstacles, the landing pattern is left hand traffic. This always-turning-left approach allows the pilot to keep the runway in sight during all phases of landing (downwind, base and final approach).

The landing phase is visually interesting and a little unnerving at first. You can't see over the nose when the airplane is pitching up. Instead, you are taught to use peripheral vision, keeping the nose lined up with the middle of the runway while relying on visual cues at the extreme end of your vision for left/right guidance. It's all gentle movements here; minor corrections on the yoke and slight taps on the rudder pedals to keep things true and straight.

As I kept focused on the runway, I thought I saw the burned-out hulk of a DC-3 on my left and remains of a twin-engine Piper on my right. The plane continued to lose airspeed before settling down gently on the dirt and gravel runway. I applied the brakes, bringing us to a stop in what I estimated was a 2,400-foot-long strip. I exhaled deeply, realizing I had been holding my breath for the last 30 seconds.

"Look," said Vince as I shut the plane down. "It's Nelson."

Indeed, it was. Mouth full of white teeth and grinning like a Cheshire cat, running up to the plane.

"Mahn," he said, "You bring da bluebird in sweet, jus like a bird."

"Thank you, Nelson," I answered. "But what about those other planes I saw on the side of the runway?"

"I guess dem not so good a pilot like you," he replied. "We have to push dem off da runway."

"How long have they been here?"

"Oh, long time," he said scratching his head. "Maybe five years[49]. Come on, we getcha loaded and outta here very fas."

As if on cue, a pickup truck appeared out the bush and drove toward us. The bales were in the back and handled by two Jamaicans. They were shrink-wrapped in a heavy-duty woven poly material not unlike some of those gigantic hay bales that dot the Midwest landscape.

---

[49]   I gathered a few facts in the coming weeks. This strip had been in operation for almost ten years. Although Air Traffic Control might have been ignorant of its existence, the Army was not. True or not, I was told they got paid $10,000 to not fly their Huey attack helicopter on certain days of the week. It seems everybody was in on these arrangements.

Before they loaded each bale on the airplane, they did the most curious thing. I couldn't understand it at the time but mere hours later it saved us from the law.

With a rag and whisk broom, they wiped down each bale with the precision of a scrub nurse, ensuring there was no external residue before putting it inside the plane. When finished, the plane was utterly stuffed. Vince had to move his seat fully forward to accommodate the load, interfering with my control yoke. It was going to be a tight squeeze all the way home.

"Jah look out for you mahn," Nelson said as they returned to the truck and disappeared into the bush.

Firing up the engine, I back taxied to the south end and prepared for takeoff. I hadn't looked at performance charts and it would not have mattered what they said. We were committed. Although we were over gross weight, we remained within the safety margins that engineers and test pilots' factor into every design.

"Here goes nothing," I said to Vince as I held the brakes, advancing the throttle to maximum power. Letting the engine build up speed for ten seconds, I released the brakes, and we started trundling heavily down the runway.

You can feel this even on commercial airplanes. The heavy thumping of the gear, the ground going by slowly. Faster and faster, the gear sound gets softer and less violent. Then that magic moment when you can feel the plane begin to get light, wanting to break free of the earth. Lighter and lighter, faster and faster. Will we use up all the runway? Will we ever take off? Then it happens. You are flying.

I used most of the runway before breaking ground and beginning a gentle climb, gaining speed ever so slowly until the airspeed indicated 120 mph. We leveled off at 200 feet and headed straight north. I suspect that every farmer and local citizen knew the exact nature of a foreign-registered airplane flying towards the sea at such an altitude.

I imagined some young Jamaican children watching us go by, waving colorful scarfs in the wind and wishing us god speed. That image in itself may give you an idea of the depth of my delusion.

We approached the coastline and left Jamaica behind, still hugging the water and headed on course to Cuba.

"Fuck, we did it!" Vince said excitedly. "We actually did it."

"Well, Phase one anyway," I reflected looking at the flight instruments. "We've got four hours to go. I still gotta find Cuba and get us over the corridor in one piece. I'll feel a little better when we are on that last leg."

In 30 minutes, we were approximately 60 miles away from Jamaica. I felt confident enough to climb back to our assigned altitude. We would enter Cuban airspace at 8,500 feet and be free to descend at our discretion once we were back over open water.

An image kept popping into my head that I couldn't quite dismiss. It involved Cuban air traffic control getting suspicious and sending up a couple fighter jets for a closer look. I imagined them sneaking up on us from behind and seeing two little pinheads sticking out from a plane stuffed full of pot. They would back off and line up behind our tail.

I wouldn't hear the tone of their missile lock as it acquired the target. It would be a quick act as the missile ripped into the little Cessna and tore it to shreds. If still conscious, I would assume a standard freefall position until impact with the water. I would bounce, but perhaps not as high as if on the land.

"Splash One," the fighter pilot would say, and the best laid plans of mice and men would disappear into the sea.

None of that happened. We flew over Cuba without incident. I began to look for that invisible pivot point over the water, that navigation fix informing me to make one final course change and head directly for Marathon.

"What's the boat look like Vince?" I asked over the reassuring noise of the motor.

"Hell, I don't know," he replied. "Russ said it's white. I guess we'll know it by the light signals he gives us. And maybe because he is circling."

This was not an insignificant detail to be thinking about. Those who have spent time in The Keys might appreciate our dilemma: there is more than one boat out on the water at any given time, some of them even circling for no apparent reason. Almost all of them are painted white.

Four hours after leaving Jamaica, we got into contact with Center and began our slow descent towards Marathon. At ten miles out we got worried. The sun was getting low on the horizon and Vince spotted dozens upon dozens of boats in the water.

"Oh my god," he said as the realization hit us. "How do we know which boat to drop to?"

As we got within three miles of Marathon the panic hit us full on. We thought we could see a boat flashing some kind of light at us, but uncertainty hit us both. It may have been circling, or not. I knew I could not land with a plane load full of pot but was not willing to just drop the load anywhere. I panicked, turned off both the transponder and radio and dove down for a closer look.

At the time, I was unaware that turning off the transponder and going radio-silent were exactly the kind of behavior that put Customs on full alert.

We circled a likely boat twice at 200 feet and a series of lights blinked in our direction.

"I think that's him," Vince said weakly. Lacking a more concrete identification of the boat, we began the drop process. Somebody was getting six bales.

Vince propped the door open with one bale against the lower door sill. It created a tremendous amount of wind resistance for the airplane but allowed him to shove the bales out one by one. As the last grouper left the plane, I climbed back into the traffic pattern and turned on my radio and transponder.

"Nine-Alpha-Quebec is with you for landing Marathon," I said.

When Tower asked where I had been for the past five minutes, I told them I had radio problems. It was a lie no one remotely considered believing.

"Nine-Alpha-Quebec, cleared to land."

We touched down just as the sun was sitting. Tower cleared us of the active runway and instructed me to park at the Customs ramp. As I taxied in, a lineman was waving his light sticks, showing me where to park. Next to him was someone in a uniform. My heart sank.

As soon as I shut down the engine and completed my post-flight checklist, he approached my door.

"You are suspected of transporting drugs," he said. "Please step out of the plane."

Vince and I deplaned at the same time. For reasons I did not fully understand, Vince was allowed to leave - and did so with great haste.

The officer immediately headed to the plane and zeroed in on my cockpit floorboards. Using his flashlight, he began to scan for signs of pot. He spotted some round pebbles that he must have thought were pot seeds. As he raked them into an envelope, I looked over his shoulder.

"Those are pebbles," I said. And they were.

In a startling flash of clarity, I understood why the Jamaicans were so fastidious about dusting off the bales. Their actions ensured that not a single trace of pot could be found on the airplane.

After a fruitless search of a few minutes, he turned and said, "come with me. There is someone flying in to meet you."

I waited perhaps 15 minutes in their interrogation room, alternatively thinking things were okay and then remembering I was in possession of a stolen airplane. Holy shit. This was not the scenario I imagined a few weeks ago. I had once been in a Mexican jail way down south and was remembering the horror of that brief incarceration.

When I heard the whine of Pratt & Whitney engines taxing in, I had a pretty good idea what was going on. They were bringing in their Citation C-550, a specially modified U.S. Customs jet with an array of sensors and secret radios designed to catch smugglers. They had made a special trip over from Homestead just for me.

The agent came through the door, Ray Ban Aviators resting on his nose. Slender, all business and dressed in a dark green jumpsuit, he sat down and began asking me questions. Deciding to play the equal, I pulled my Ran Ban

Aviators out and faced him. Who was I, where is my license, what were you doing in Jamaica, why did you drop off radar and who owned the airplane?

Again, without leaning too much on the divine, I had a bulletproof answer for every question including why the N number was not showing up on the FAA registry. I was absolutely unfazed and a stone-cold liar.

"It's brand new," I said, "and belongs to our flying club. We just haven't had time to register it. I've got all the logbooks and paperwork if you want to see it."

It was dark in the office, and he still had his Aviators on. He pulled out a cigarette and struck a match. I pulled out my Dunhills and lit up as well. We sat there for perhaps a few minutes in silence, looking each other over.

Finally, he removed his sunglasses. I did the same.

"Son," he said looking me straight in the eyes, "I can't figure out if you are the smartest kid I ever met or the dumbest."

"Without a doubt, sir," I said in a gesture of deep introspection, "I am one of the dumbest human beings you will ever meet."

With that, he released me.

———————————

I walked out of the terminal and headed down the street. I knew Vince and Alex were waiting somewhere in the darkness. I walked a block south, headed towards A1A when a headlight flashed me.

"Oh my god," Vince exclaimed, "what just happened? What about the plane?"

"He had to let me go," I replied. "They couldn't find a trace in the plane. I guess that's what Nelson's guys were doing back on the strip. That N number change saved our ass."

"Great job," said Alex. "Vince told me you guys made a successful drop. I gotta tell you that you're the youngest pilot who's ever pulled this off."

"Have you heard from Russ?" I asked.

"No," replied Alex, "but he'll be back at the docks early tomorrow morning. I'll get in touch with him then. This calls for a celebration."

I told Vince and Alex I would go out with them but must leave early the next morning. The plane was seriously overdue, and I didn't want the Feds checking any deeper into a fake N number.

We arrived at one of the local tiki bars and settled down for a round of beers and oysters. I was into my third beer when I heard my name being yelled from across the room.

It was an old friend from my hometown. I knew he had migrated down to The Keys a few years back but had no idea he landed in Marathon. We hoisted a few rounds together and I dodged his questions about what I was doing in town.

"Incredible," said Vince as my friend left. "I have never met anybody who seems to know someone everywhere we go. How is that?"

"I don't know," I said, "but it seems to work out that way, doesn't it?"

Alex had gotten up during our conversation and wandered off. He came back a few minutes later with his friend Axel. We made quick introductions. Axel complimented me on the drop and again told me I was the youngest pilot to complete a drop without training. I was somewhat flattered, but taken back by the magnitude of what I had just accomplished.

Instead of going back to Johnny's house, Axel put us up for the night in his mobile home. He and Alex were Key West natives, and reminisced about the coldest night of their lives when the temperature approached 40°F.

"We had the oven on, and every burner lit on the stove," he reminisced. "We still just about froze to death."

I listened with amusement but noted how different life must be in a tropical environment versus the harsh Midwest climate I had experienced most of my life. After another beer, I snagged a sleeping bag from the closet and headed over to the couch. I wanted to be out the door early the next morning and get Bluebird back to the FBO.

Fueling up at Marathon the next morning, I had just a few minutes to speak with Vince.

"Did the drop go as planned?" I asked. "What did Johnny say?"

"Alex told me not to talk to Johnny. Said he is probably deep, deep in audits and shouldn't be disturbed. I guess the drop went okay. Alex didn't say anything else about it."

"I have to get the plane back Vince," I replied. "Are you coming with me?"

"No, I'm going to stick around for a few days."

"Okay, but what about my payment?"

"I've got five grand on me now. I'll pay you the other fifteen when we get back home."

"Sure," I said with implicit trust in Vince, "so long as it's not more than a week."

Vince handed me a fat envelope of $100 dollar bills. I counted the money and put it in my shirt pocket alongside my Dunhills. We embraced, and I headed into the FBO to get an idea of the weather.

The forecast was not good. A system was moving in from the west and expected to blanket the entire region with heavy weather over the next five days. The farthest I could get towards home was Dallas. I thought I owed Shane at the FBO a call to explain a slight delay.

"DUDE," he said when he realized who was on the other end, "we are in so much trouble. They know the plane is missing. Where the fuck are you? And where the fuck is the airplane?"

"How did they find out?" I asked more out of curiosity than need.

"I don't know," he continued. "Somebody was checking the lock box keys against an inventory. All I know is that they discovered one set of keys is missing. Right now, they are checking area FBOs to see if somehow the plane got parked there by accident. You have got to get back now!"

I said I was in Florida watching a Space Shuttle Launch, and that it was going to be at least another five days before the plane made it back.

"Fuck you," he said as he slammed the phone in my ear.

As I taxied out, I remembered a wedding that I was expected to attend in a few days. Even more complications. The best I could do was park the plane in Dallas, catch a commercial flight back home and return in a few days for Bluebird.

I lifted off the strip at Marathon, flying over the water towards Marco Island and the southwest tip of Florida. From the air it is possible to see the Everglades stretching towards infinity, in a land the Indians called Pa-hay-Okee.

In times before the white man arrived, almost one-third of the state drained southward from Lake Okeechobee down to this sea of grass, home to an almost uncountable variety of wildlife. Even from this shallow altitude, I could see endless pools of water reflecting off the early morning sunlight as far as the eye could see.

Flying slightly offshore and parallel with the coast, I flew over the sparkling islands of Captiva and Sanibel. Farther up the coast came Sarasota and Clearwater. Keeping out of the heavily trafficked airspace surrounding these cities, I made my way north in Bluebird at a steady two miles per minute.

Passing over Cedar Key and angling back over the Gulf, I passed the historic fishing town of Apalachicola and from there continued northward over solid ground.

Looking at the maps I had acquired during the trip, it occurred to me that the Cuba/Jamaica chart might be a bit incriminating. I did the only rational thing possible, opening up the pilot side window and tossing it into the slipstream.

I had not counted on the map unfolding as it exited the airplane. In doing so, it became a sort of parachute and quickly wrapped itself around the tail section's horizontal stabilizer. I thought perhaps that a few movements of the control yoke would either release it or tear it to shreds, but neither thing happened.

For 50 minutes, I would glance back occasionally and see the map still holding on, reminding me of that skydiving student who would not let go of the strut. As I approached for landing in the uncontrolled Alabama airport, I called out my intentions.

"Nine-Alpha-Quebec on a three-mile final for landing, runway one-nine," I announced over the radio.

As is the case in many of these small airports, the common frequency – known as Unicom – is manned by the local FBO. They may or may not respond to your radio call, and local aviators will also use this frequency to announce their position to other aircraft in the area.

"Nine-Alpha-Quebec," came the response, *"winds one-four at one-eight-zero, no known traffic in the pattern. Are you requiring services?"*

"Nine-Alpha-Quebec, affirmative. I would like fuel."

It was another beautiful approach with winds coming almost straight down the runway. I pulled on carb heat to keep the engine from icing up while reducing power and adding flaps. Gentle, gentle, gentle on the controls and kiss the earth with your tires.

I taxied off the far end of the active runway, pulled over, reduced power to idle and set the emergency brake. Exiting the plane, I ran back to the tail and gathered the map, hoping no one at the FBO saw me.

The lineman was waiting with his wands and flagged me to a stop. Getting out the plane after four hours flying, it felt good to stretch. Thank god I didn't have to pee in flight and haul out a urine-colored jug in front of him.

"We don't see that too often," he said taking my fuel order.

"See what?" I asked.

"Maps stuck on the tail," he said without editorial comment.

Lifting off again with a full tank of fuel, I headed toward Dallas and the small airport I had chosen just east of their major airspace area. My old friend Rob, whom I had contacted earlier in the day, was waiting to pick me up.

"Really?" he said looking at my outfit. "Do you have a change of clothes?"

I had not considered my clothes at all. But when I looked in the mirror I cringed. A sort of crappy light blue, long-sleeved fake rhinestone cowboy shirt, old gym shorts and a funky pair of tennis shoes apparently from the DAV. Of course, my Ray Bans and Dunhills were stuffed into the only pockets I had. That and a wad of $100s. Quite the look.

Rob drove me to his loft apartment. Situated in an old warehouse district, the space was light and airy. It was a perfect spot for his photo studio, and his cameras and lights were always ready for the next fashion model to show up. And here I was, ready for a session.

We were old friends, reaching back to grade school and swimming parties at the country club. In high school, I taught him how to use a camera. Within the year he had leapfrogged my abilities and become my teacher. Two years later, he was shooting professionally[50]. Like my early boss at the newspaper, Rob had an extraordinary eye for detail.

"I've got to make a portrait of this for posterity," he said loading his Hasselblad with a Polaroid back. Adjusting the camera and lighting, he took a photo and checked for proper exposure using the instant print feature of the Polaroid. Satisfied with the settings, he swapped the back for a standard roll of Pan-X and made a few images.

---

[50] It was during this time that he and I were asked to show up at a local jail. Something about unpaid traffic tickets we had both acquired and needed to pay or face jail time. We were booked and fingerprinted in some kind of over-the-top display by another Roger Ramjet type.

Surveying this officer's studio setup, I noticed a long flash cord running from his camera to the remote lighting. Without being noticed, I used my feet to unplug the flash cord extension as it snaked across the floor. I told Rob I was going to make the guy say "damn" when he pressed the shutter.

Sure enough, he pressed the shutter, nothing flashed, and he said "damn." Rob began to laugh and officer Ramjet shot him a hard look. "You think this is funny son?" he asked. Rob shook his head while the officer fiddled around for a full five minutes before discovering that his synch cord had somehow come loose on the floor.

"I'll pick the best one and have it ready when you come back," he said.

After a quick lunch, he dropped me off at Love Field. I rushed to the counter and purchased a one-way ticket back to the Midwest. With no luggage to check and a wad of hundred-dollar bills stuffed in my shirt pocket, I paid cash and jogged toward the gate.

I arrived just as the stewardess was making final boarding call. She took my ticket and gave me a hard look from head to toe.

"Well, you win," she said with a straight face.

"Win what?" I asked in sincerity.

"The worst dressed award."

I laughed hard, feeling like a master of the world. I had, in fact, just won another round with the law. Perhaps my countenance showed.

"But," she concluded without a hint of sarcasm, "you look like you want to have a good time. I have just the seat for you."

She marched me down the aisle and sat me between two very attractive young women.

"Now buy them a drink," she commanded.

"I never buy ladies a drink unless I know their names," I rebuffed.

Two pairs of hands shot out like arrows, and they quickly introduced themselves. We spent the entire flight in animated conversation, enhanced by two bottles of wine whose content seemed to magically disappear.

Trouble On the Home Front

"How was the rocket launch?" my mother asked as we surveyed the wedding reception crowd.

I almost forgot the lie I had been telling everyone; that I had rented a plane and flown down to Florida to watch a space shuttle blast off.

How can you lie to your mother? With a deep sense of chagrin, I suppose.

"Unbelievable," I said with little more comment. I always heard the more you lie the deeper the tangle gets. I was trying to keep this fabrication to its bare bones, but relatives at the wedding kept poking and prodding. I did my best to accommodate them while sticking to a simple script.

"Everybody is having so much fun," my mom continued. "And look at your dad, he's really enjoying himself. I haven't seen him this affectionate in forever."

"Don't drink the punch, mom," I confessed. "I spiked it with grain alcohol[51]. Dad is happy because he's drunk."

She looked at me aghast and then laughed. We were in the middle of a no-alcohol crowd, uptight, upright and, unknowingly, getting collectively hammered.

I watched as a stern aunt, farm-raised and serious in countenance, began to glow. She headed back to the punch bowl for another helping.

"Best punch I've ever had," she said to no one in particular.

Another aunt, life of any party and no stranger to drink, was having difficulty judging the distance from her body to a support column. I watched as she tried to act nonchalant and lean against something solid.

---

[51] Much like high octane av gas, this distillate tips the scales at 190 proof, or 95% pure alcohol.

Only trouble was the column was a bit farther away than she anticipated. She leaned into it, leaned a bit more against dead air and came crashing abruptly to a stop. Startled, she looked around - and satisfied that no one saw her - finished her punch.

All the while the conversation level kept increasing. At first it was a gentle murmur, and then it got progressively louder until the drunken hordes were yelling at each other, each voice competing against an ever-rising volume. I left the marbled reception hall, seeking quiet and solitude on a nearby fire escape.

On Monday I would need to get back down to Dallas and pick up Bluebird. I needed clear weather and someone to help change the registration and install a new tachometer. And probably some black paint on the propeller to hide pits and dings acquired in Jamaica.

After the wedding I headed over to my folk's house and was surprised to get a call from Vince.

"There's a little problem with the money on my end," he said. "Johnny told me he can front you the cash out of my future proceeds, but you gotta come back to Miami to pick it up."

That was not an insurmountable obstacle. I needed to fly back down to Dallas anyway, so perhaps an initial stop in Miami would be no problem.

"Alright Vince," I said. "I think I can catch a flight out on Tuesday if you can pick me up at the airport."

Later that night I got an additional call from Axel. I guess he got my folk's number from Vince.

"Somebody named Axis on the phone for you," my dad yelled.

"Hey man," Axel wanted to know, "can you come back to The Keys and fly for me next week?"

I was still confused about how all the back shop pieces fit together between the players, but didn't question it deeply.

"I don't know," I told him. "I had only planned on this being a one-time shot."

"Well think about it," he finished. "This might turn out to be a real lucrative deal for you."

After the weekend wedding, I said my goodbyes to the family and headed back to my apartment a few hundred miles away. Flush with some folding money courtesy of Vince, I did what any irresponsible young man would do. I headed to the audio store.

Our college town was able to support a high-end audio shop and I would often show up just to listen to their Martin-Logan electrostatic speakers. Unlike any other speakers with a box enclosure, these Monoliths sandwiched a thin Mylar film between two transparent metal screens.

You could literally see thru these speakers, and when powered by one of their massive amps, they would transport you right into the music. It was almost incomprehensible that those things which did not look at all like speakers were producing such astonishing clarity and presence.

That was not in my budget range, but a very, very nice Danish Bang & Olufsen system was calling my name. Their flagship receiver, the Beomaster 3000, was so different and unique in design that it ended up being displayed in the Museum of Modern Art. I coupled that with their top-of-the-line speakers and turntable.

To round it off, I made a comprehensive dash through the record store and picked up about 100 new albums. It was all I could do to get everything loaded into my MGB.

Back at my apartment, I had enough time to unbox the system and give it an initial listen. Stunning, stunning clarity[52] coming from that low-mass needle of the turntable, rotating at 33 1/3 rpm as my world likewise began to spin out of control.

———————————

---

[52]   "You have a really, really nice stereo," my downstairs neighbor said one time. "I can hear every note, every cymbal." What the law student was trying to tell me was to turn the volume way, way down so she could hear herself think.

Two days later, I left my apartment and caught a direct flight back to Miami; this time dressed to avoid winning any sort of award. Vince and Alex met me at the terminal, still with no sign of Johnny.

"We lost the load," Alex offered as I squeezed into the back of his Alfa.

"You dropped it all over the place and Russ only got one bale. Somebody is out there now with a boat full of groupers. It's a tight crowd here in Marathon. We'll figure out who picked them up and get it back. But for now, don't say a fucking word to Johnny. He doesn't know about any of this. I told him you flew home without a load."

The loss of the load was apparently news to Vince as well.

"Shit Alex," Vince said in a real panic. "I'm on the hook for this. This is my deal. Who's going to pay Nelson?"

"Don't worry," Alex continued, "Nelson is covered, and I'll get this figured out. Just keep your mouth shut."

It was the same drive out of Miami, down Card Sound Road and intersecting the Overseas Highway as we headed towards Marathon. But this time instead of seeing a spectacular ocean view, my vision kept narrowing.

"I'll see you guys in a few days," Alex said as he dropped us off at Vince's motel. "I got some stuff I gotta take care of."

"Shit," Vince reflected inside the room, "this is serious; really serious. I'm on the hook for most of this. Alex told me he was sending a bale up north, but I thought it was just to get me going until the rest of the shipment arrived. Even if I could sell everything in dime bags[53], I'm still into Johnny for almost $100,000."

I didn't have any suggestions for Vince, but it confirmed my initial feelings about Alex. Although I never trusted him, we could be forgiven for not knowing how Johnny's finance and distribution network was structured.

---

[53] The smallest amount of pot typically sold at the street level with a value of $10. This would require Vince cutting out all his middle-men distributors and selling directly to their end-users. Not a smart move to undercut your own network.

110

It wasn't our business to understand the shadowy and byzantine network, and it was compartmentalized by design so that one broken link would not bring down the whole organization. Who was Axel in this? Who was Russ back in Jamaica? What was Nelson's involvement? Somehow, I thought dealing with Johnny would have been much more straightforward.

We spent the afternoon getting progressively more worried, and a call from Johnny didn't help.

"Hey Vince," he said casually, "I'm going to pick you guys up around six. Let's go have dinner and see if we can't get a load this time."

The black Audi wheeled into our parking lot right on time. Johnny knocked on the door and invited himself in. Still in black, he was the same taut, ice-cold persona I remembered from our first meeting.

"Let's go get some supper down the road," he volunteered. "I'm buying."

As we got into the backseat, I noticed a new face up front. No introductions were made but this guy looked like a hard muscle enforcer, and he remained mute as Vince and Johnny spoke. I was listening to the tenor of their conversation, and it felt artificial; like two Spartans in a ring angling for advantage.

This whole charade seemed like madness to me. Although there might not be honor among thieves, I wanted no part of this deception with Johnny. I have always tried to live a transparent life, as if people could read me like an open book. Perhaps some of Bob's juju was rubbing off on me, because I could feel Johnny reading every line of every page of this great lie.

Something internal told me he wanted to see how deep the hook was set before reeling us in. And the muscle up front looked every bit the part of a mafia hit man.

"I made the drop," I said from the backseat behind Johnny. I could see his neck stiffen.

"He spilled the beans," said muscle from the front seat. "He spilled the beans."

111

"What the fuck?" said Johnny.

"I made the drop to somebody named Russ," I offered. "Three hundred pounds."

We drove on in silence for a few minutes more before pulling into a nondescript and ill-lit motel.

"Get out of the car," he said. "Into the motel now."

As we entered the room and turned on the dingy lights, it felt like an interrogation session was about to begin. We were ordered to sit down at the table. I imagined the worst and Johnny confirmed it.

"I knew you flew the fucking load," he exploded. "I know everything that goes on here in The Keys," and he slammed his fist against the table. "I brought you here to kill you, Vince. And I may still. Now tell me exactly what happened."

We relayed every detail; our initial meeting with Axel, the multiple day delays once in Jamaica and driving to Kingston to meet with Russ.

"You met with Russ in Jamaica?" Johnny screamed. "God damn it. I'll kill that motherfucker. And Alex was with him?"

"We didn't talk with Russ," Vince offered. "We just saw him in Kingston and thought he was a part of your crew. How could we know?"

"You have sunk me," Johnny said looking at Vince.

From what I was piecing together, Alex had gone to Jamaica, used Johnny's credit line to get the pot and dropped it to his friends Russ and Axel. He then proceeded to tell Johnny that we had never picked up a load in Montego Bay.

Whether or not the pot was lost at sea was a secondary point. Johnny was on the hook for 300 pounds that he didn't possess. Alex swore to Vince that the pot disappeared. And Johnny was looking for a target of opportunity since Alex had failed to show up at the meeting.

"You know who's responsible for paying Nelson?" Johnny asked. "I am. And that means you too Vince. I swear to god, you're a dead man."

Reaching behind his back, he brought out a 9mm Baretta and leveled it at Vince's head. I noted at least the hammer had not been cocked. And I noted another thing. I was not the object of Johnny's rage. I had come clean in the car. Perhaps this honesty saved my life. But Vince was looking at eternity and shaking almost uncontrollably. Muscle looked ready to spring as well.

"Let me redeem Vince," I said.

"What are you talking about?" Johnny responded, lowering the gun slightly and looking at me.

"Look, this has always been strictly a business deal for me," I offered. "I'm just a pilot, but I'll fly another load for you without cost if you'll spare Vince's life."

Johnny lowered the gun.

From the time I met him, we seemed to have shared a more business-like perspective on the whole operation. He appeared to be considering the ramifications of killing us both on the spot or trying to recover some of his losses.

"Alright," Johnny said tucking the pistol back into his waist, "it's a deal." But looking at Vince he added, "this isn't over yet."

"Find my cousin[54]," he said turning to muscle. "He's a dead mother fucker. And get Axel and Russ while you're at it."

---

[54] By this time, Alex knew the jig was up. Blood being thicker than water, Johnny did not kill Alex or even harm him. But Alex knew Johnny needed a few days to cool off, and because Alex owned the only silver Alfa GTV on the island, it wasn't hard to spot his general location. Alex did the only logical thing he could and climbed up high in the mango trees, suspending a hammock in the branches; laying low for two days with the gecko lizards while tropical breezes provided a sort of cooling effect to all parties involved.

With that, Johnny led us out of the room and back to his car. We drove north in silence. Muscle was staring straight ahead while Vince was attempting to hide his shaking hands, clutching them tightly. I was trying to process the import of what just transpired, and what could have happened. Holy shit.

Eventually, Johnny turned on the radio but tension in the car overwhelmed any sound coming out of the speakers. Returning to our motel seemed to take an eternity, and I kept wondering if we were being driven to an execution spot.

After an hour of driving, we rounded the corner to our motel. Perhaps we would live after all. I got out of the car and looked at Johnny.

"Thank you," I said.

"Don't fuck this up," he nodded. "You're a stand-up guy. Maybe we can keep doing business."

Back inside our motel room, Vince was still shaking. "I need a drink and a biscuit[55]," he said, starting a daily trend that would impair his judgment from here on out.

"Wow Vince," I said, "this isn't exactly what I had in mind when I said yes. You know how close we came back there? I think Johnny really meant it."

"Oh, he meant it all right," Vince reflected. "Thank you. I owe you my life."

Up until now I had never considered the depth of that statement. What does it mean to step into redemption for another human being?

Is this what happens when a Marine falls on a grenade, saving the lives of his buddies? Is this another chapter from that terrible story of *Sophie's Choice?*

---

[55]   Quaaludes. In the early 1980s this illegal depressant was so popular in Miami that it was referred to as a 'disco biscuit.'

Did Jesus knowingly step onto a cross to redeem not just one man but an entire humanity? Is such a story even believable?

And how do the redeemed live with themselves afterwards? What can they do to honor such a gesture, either real or imagined? How do you live the rest of your life in debt, and what does repayment look like?

There's a classic line from the movie *Titanic* when Rose and the survivors are in lifeboats, having just witnessed the great ship sink beneath the waves and all the screams for help have gone quiet.

"Afterwards," Rose reflected, "the 700 people in the boats had nothing to do but wait. Wait to live. Wait to die. Wait for an absolution that would never come."

Vince and I waited in that motel room, a quietness descending over us like the holy ghost. We were both offered a sort of redemption, but not the kind spelled out in morality plays.

We would fly again.

In Like-new Condition

The next morning Vince handed me another $2,000 partial payment for what we now referred to as the '*lost load*.' That still left me way short of the mythical jackpot. In addition, I was going to have to find another plane to fly back to Jamaica. It certainly would not be borrowed this time. In fact, I would be paying for rental costs out of my own pocket.

"Vince," I said as he handed over the money, "this should cover my costs for the next airplane rental, but what about the rest? Where is my $13,000?"

"I don't know," he said in a worried voice. "I'll figure something out. Maybe I can pay you in product."

"Not what I am looking for. I wouldn't know what to do with that amount of pot. I don't have many friends I can sell to, and it would take a long time to smoke it all."

"Just hang in there with me," he pleaded as he rummaged around his trouser pockets and pulled out another biscuit. "It'll be okay when we get the next load delivered. I can pay you then."

We discussed our next steps. Of paramount importance was getting Bluebird back home and tucked away into the endless rows of new airplanes. But all this flying around had put hours on the tachometer. Unlike shady used car salesmen who would roll the miles backwards on a speedometer before resale, I needed a replacement instrument.

I put a call in to my mechanic friend, requesting he order a tach and vinyl registration numbers for a planned arrival the next few days. Again, he agreed to help me without question or comment. In doing so, I became further indebted to him on favors I would never be able to repay.

Vince agreed to stay in The Keys while I returned Bluebird and sourced another airplane, preferably one with more weight-carrying capability. I needed to be back within seven days to keep to Johnny's recently announced schedule.

Heading back to the Miami airport, I caught one of the frequent non-stop flights to Dallas and made my way to the back, where smoking was allowed.

Some airline executive, probably a former vice president of R.J. Reynolds Tobacco, had convinced everybody that my smoke would stay in the back of the plane and not end up in the non-smoking section. This executive had probably not read the maintenance manual, which clearly showed how all the air was mixed together and recirculated again and again.

The plus side of sitting in the rear section was that it was seldom occupied. Almost like having a business jet all to myself. I pulled out a Dunhill and opened the shade to see the early morning sky. Oops, I forgot. In the back when you open the shade all you see is the engine nacelle.

I tried to think through how to get Bluebird back on the line unnoticed. By now everyone at the FBO knew an airplane had gone missing. They didn't know where or when, but it was certainly not among the living. I decided the best I could do was to return it at night, leave the keys on the dash like an Enterprise rental, and hope no one had my credit card information.

It was not much of a plan, I thought as the constant whine of the Pratt & Whitney engines lulled me to sleep, but it was the only one I had.

Upon landing, I caught a taxi back to the nearby airfield where I had stashed Bluebird the week before.

Walking into the FBO, a smoking-hot desk attendant asked what she could do for me. Humm??

"I've got Nine-Alpha-Quebec on the ramp," I replied. "I need to pay my tie-down fees[56] and get topped off."

---

[56] Almost every airport has provisions for securing your aircraft with metal tie-down loops built into the parking ramp. You position your airplane so that each wing is over a tie-down loop and the tail is over a similar loop. Ropes or chains are then used to connect the airplane to the earth.

If properly secured, a plane can withstand almost any storm or wind gusts without damage. Every FBO charges a daily fee for this tie-down. A more expensive option is to house your airplane overnight inside their hangar. In this world, nobody flies for free.

"Yes sir," she said with just the right hint of a suggestive smile. "Would you be Bill Mahoney?"

Oh shit. Was this a trick question? Time to confess all my sins and give up?

'Who wants to know?' is what I wanted to say.

"Yes ma'am," I answered. "Why?"

"A gentleman left this package for you yesterday," she explained while reaching under the counter to retrieve it.

Thinking about how many ways I might be incriminated; I tucked the parcel under my arm and headed out the door. With my back to her window, I opened the plain brown box to find a beautiful studio portrait of myself taken a week earlier by Rob.

I don't mean to imply the subject was beautiful. In fact, as I gazed at the portrait, I laughed at the ridiculous clown costume[57] I had worn to the airport. The beauty came from Rob's eye; the lighting, the texture, the quality of the print and the mounted frame.

I placed it beside me in the co-pilot seat. Some people say god is their co-pilot. I was sticking with Bill Mahoney.

I walked back into the office and paid my fuel bill. Stepping into the pilot's lounge, I picked up their dedicated phone and called the FAA for a weather briefing. The big storm system had cleared out and it looked like VFR conditions all the way north.

I ran my calculations for the trip and determined that I could make the flight back home without an intermediate fuel stop. That early experience running out of gas made a lasting, and positive, impression on me. I headed to the bathroom to empty my bladder before embarking on a four-hour exercise in endurance.

---

[57] This image hangs on my wall even today. It still makes me laugh to think about the flight attendant's impromptu award.

Entering the stall, I took out an ink pen and decided to add to the door's graffiti. On impulse I drew an image of Kilroy, the ubiquitous cartoon image made popular by World War II servicemen. Thinking it needed some kind of new tag line, I wrote beneath it, "Bill Mahoney was here."

Bill Mahoney was here

I walked back to the ramp and prepared for the flight home. On a new airplane, a pre-flight inspection might seem as unnecessary as checking the oil level on a brand-new car at every fill up. Perhaps it is.

Yet walking around Bluebird, checking every visible nut and bolt for tightness, wiggling each control surface, tugging on the prop, checking tires for proper inflation, making sure flaps extend and navigation lights work, gave me a sense of oneness with the airplane.

Maybe that's the entire thing in a nutshell. At its core, it is a ritual. Like an Eastern Orthodox priest swinging incense over the congregants, pilots are touching the airplane, bonding with it and seeking its blessing before another magical flight into the ether. And on rare occasion, finding something that needs immediate attention.

Bluebird, however, needed no attention. She was ready for flight, and I taxied down the ramp, positioning her for engine run-up prior to takeoff. Of all the pre-flight checks, this is perhaps the most important. Line the plane up into the wind, set the brakes and move the throttle forward until the tachometer reads 1700 rpm.

Test the dual ignition system, making sure each independent magneto can power the engine if its backup fails. Test for carb heat effectiveness, make sure all the engines' gauges are in the green and operating properly. Move the throttle back to idle and contact the tower.

With their permission, it's onto the active runway for takeoff. Smooth application of power, looking straight down the nose at the runway center line; small corrections on the rudder pedals to keep it tracking straight, aileron adjustments as the airspeed builds and then that feeling of lightness as the ship builds up speed.

Pulling back gently on the yoke to raise the nose slightly, sensing the air resistance slacken, feeling the impact of tires against the runway diminish until finally she breaks free and leaps gently into the air.

It's tricky business now. You are flying, but just barely. Give physics its due. Keep the plane low off the runway and let her build up some speed. Now, gently, increase back pressure on the yoke and pitch the nose up a bit. Watch as airspeed builds slowly, and the climb rate increases. Now you're flying and you watch in your peripheral vision as the runway falls below you.

As I gained altitude and exited the Dallas-controlled airspace, I was released to fly on my own course. Just as there are highways for cars, there are airways for airplanes. Unlike a car, you are not required to travel on an airway. If you do, however, there are very specific rules of the road that must be followed.

I was choosing to fly homeward in 'uncontrolled' airspace. The rules here are few and simple, but one way in which head-on collisions are avoided is the 'east is odd, west is even' mnemonic.

Think of it like a divided highway where traffic is separated. But in the air, this highway is turned sideways. Eastbound traffic is relegated to odd altitudes (1,500; 3,500; 5,500; 7,500; 9,500, etc). Westbound traffic is supposed to fly at even altitudes (2,500; 4,500; 6,500; 8,500, etc...).

If everybody follows the rules, you will never have a head-on collision and traffic will always be either safely above or below your flight path. Because I was flying in a northeast direction, I chose an altitude of 7,500 feet, kept my radio on to listen for pilot-to-pilot chatter and continually scanned the skies, watching for traffic that might not be adhering to the rules.

Perhaps one other thing deserves explanation, and it concerns the discussion about reporting altitudes. There are two ways to talk about altitude, either AGL (Above Ground Level) or MSL (Mean Sea Level).

Skydivers only talk about AGL. They could care less about how high a landing zone is above sea level. Before taking off, they will reset their altimeters on the ground to read 0 feet. In freefall, when their altimeters enter the red zone at 2,500 feet, they know it's time to deploy their parachute. They bounce when their altimeters reach zero.

Pilots live on the other end of the spectrum and only talk about MSL. They set their 0 feet according to the sea. If you fly out of the mountains, your runway may be 6,000 feet above sea level (MSL). Pilots will make sure their altimeter reads 6,000 feet before taking off. In this way, pilots across the world are always using the same reference point.

This means that when flying at 7,500 feet MSL according to my altimeter, I may only be 4,000 feet above the ground. If I am flying over rising terrain, the distance between my airplane and the ground keeps diminishing with every mile I fly. Eventually, I might find a mountain on my flight path. Not a good thing.

But in the vast Midwest Plains, the ground is not subject to rising up and killing you. As I flew along in the moderately choppy air, the temperature had dropped[58] about 30°F and was providing for pleasant flying conditions.

Off to my left and right were beautiful cumulus clouds, each with their unique shapes and formed like irregular cotton balls. From the ground, clouds can look one-dimensional. It's only when you fly beside and between them that their three-dimensional character comes to life. And what a spectacular visual show.

Often a cloud, plain looking from one side, would explode in depth and color as you rounded a corner, the sun illuminating its every nook and cranny. It is like being on acid without the side effects. The other thing clouds provide is a reference to speed.

In blue sky, it almost appears that the airplane is suspended, and the earth turns slowly underneath it. When clouds are present, however, you get a

---

58   The air temperature consistently drops 5.4°F for every 1,000 feet you climb. This is known as the Dry Adiabatic Lapse Rate. Because small airplanes are seldom equipped with air conditioning, climbing up high in the summer months helps to mitigate what amounts to flying around in a hot tin can with greenhouse glass surrounding you on all sides. Want to lose weight? Fly at low altitudes in the Florida summer. The weight will come off in great buckets of sweat.

sense of speed and how fast you are moving. As I flew northward, the sun cast my shadow on the clouds below. My plane appeared to be rising and dipping with every change in the cloud, flying over it at frightening speed.

I watched for 40 minutes as we raced each other, Bluebird always slightly ahead and to the right of her shadow self. Finally, the clouds thinned and dissipated, breaking the illusion and leaving me floating in a sea of eternity.

After four hours of flying, I began a leisurely descent. Throttling back and adding a little carb heat as a precautionary measure, I dropped down to 3,000 feet. The air was noticeably warmer and thicker. Even the plane's controls felt this change, something that always amazed me.

At ten miles out, I dropped into pattern altitude and announced my landing intentions over the radio. There was no other traffic in the area and no one responding on the ground. It's an odd feeling, broadcasting into dead air; reminding me of those late-night DJs who talk and talk and talk in hopes that someone, somewhere is listening.

It wasn't a great landing. Certainly not the Zen experience I have described before. A stiff and gusty crosswind kept blowing me towards the runway's edge. About the time I had compensated for this drift, a new gust would hit and force me to change my angle.

I fought the landing all the way, dialing in one correction after another while the airspeed bled slowly down. Eventually, the main wheels chirped hard against pavement and the nose gear came down with a solid thunk.

Even then, it required careful attention. As I turned around and back taxied on the empty runway, I had to think about how the wind wanted to lift a wing and tip me over. They say a flight is not over until the plane is in the hangar or tied down.

I wheeled around the old fuel pump and immediately flashed back to that female pilot I saw pirouette in the exact manner some years ago. I shut the plane down, found a tie-down spot and lashed Bluebird to the earth.

I was home, but still a few hours away from the FBO of my misadventure. I needed to call Shane and check the water temperature.

"Oh my god dude, where are you," he asked in a near-hysterical voice. "And more to the point, where is the airplane?"

"How's the temperature?" I cringed even as I asked.

"It's way beyond hot," he continued, "but you may have lucked out. The FBO is being sold and everybody is busy going over the books. The current owner would rather not have a stolen airplane pop up during their negotiations, but I think you are their prime suspect. Your name keeps coming up."

"I plan on bringing the airplane back tomorrow night and just parking it on the ramp," I said. "I'll leave the keys on the floorboard. Can we meet up afterwards?"

"Hell no," he said. "I don't know anything about this, and I never want to talk to you again. I suggest you never show your face around here again. Ever. Again." And he hung up on me for a second time.

I wandered into the back shop and found my mechanic buddy. He had the vinyl registration and tachometer ready to go, and we installed them on the windy ramp. The vinyl letters looked mostly straight. He brought out a can of black spray paint and we did our best to make the prop look like it had not been dinged by rock chips from a Jamaican gravel strip.

After that, it was a very thorough cleaning in and out. I took a critical look at the Cessna, unsure if she would pass a close inspection. There were several scuff marks and discolorations on the copilot's door. These were caused by square groupers exiting the plane, and a trained eye would not consider this a factory-induced quality escape.

It was the best we could do. I thanked my mechanic friend, paid him a generous sum in cash and decided to return to the FBO that night. I wanted to put this part of the adventure behind me.

Refueled and ready to go, I yelled "clear the prop" out the hinged window and fired up Bluebird for one last time. The sun had set as I taxied out and mercifully, the wind had died down. I flew the next 90 minutes in real gratitude for what clearly seemed like divine protection.

Calling Tower on my approach into Bluebird's home base, I used a made-up N number in case they were on the hunt for a missing Cessna. After landing, I taxied to the FBO and found a vacant tie down spot. I dropped the keys on the floor and shut the door.

I took a few quick strides away from the scene of my crime before turning around, and in my own goofy way, thanked Bluebird for bringing me back home safely. The airport lights were twinkling their nighttime magic that seemed to bring out the beauty in everything. From 15 feet away she looked to be *'in Like-new Condition'*.

Heading out the back exit, I had no idea if the law would catch up with me or if somehow, I had dodged a bullet to end all bullets. My name was at least tangentially associated with a missing plane that had suddenly reappeared. Would they throw a feast like that biblical Father whose prodigal son returned, or would they cast me into a lion's den?

The only thing certain was that I must never, ever show my face again at this FBO. My name was mud and – like Lord Voldemort - could never be spoken out loud again.

A New Ride

Thinking about the seven degrees of separation and concentric circles of influence, I decided that putting a couple hundred miles between me and Bluebird would be sufficient distance to find a new airplane. The rental facility I had in mind was typical of many flight schools in that they would rent out customer's airplanes from time to time. This arrangement helped the owner make payments, and it allowed the schools to offer new, high-performance airplanes without having to own them outright.

I chose a nearly new Piper Turbo Arrow IV, a fast yet economical single engine with a turbo charger and retractable gear. Checkout was straightforward with the chief flight instructor, and my story had a more authentic ring of making a trip to Florida and back with some scuba-diving friends.

The company accepted my money order as full deposit and handed me keys with the understanding I would be back in one week. This was a promise I intended to keep.

The Piper was a different critter altogether from the Cessna. It had a top speed of 170 miles per hour, was equipped with an autopilot and had a range of nearly 700 miles. It would climb to 20,000 feet if needed and could lift off easily from a dirt strip with a full load.

I checked into an area motel for the night and called Vince.

"I got a new ride," I told him. "It's super nice and quite a bit faster than the 172. I'm flying out tomorrow morning and will be in The Keys before sunset. How are things down there?

"Well, Alex came down from the trees and is talking to Johnny again," offered Vince. "But it's still pretty tense."

"What about Axel and Russ? And before I forget, Axel called me at my folks. Did you give him the number?" I inquired.

"They can't be found," Vince said. "Even their boat has disappeared from the docks. Johnny thinks they are hiding out in Ft. Lauderdale. And yes, I slipped and gave your number to Axel. Sorry about that."

I remembered that Jimmy was working out of Ft. Lauderdale as well and wondered if they knew each other. It was a very small, if paranoid, community in which everybody appeared to be interconnected. The whole of South Florida seemed to be involved with drugs in one way or another, and the action seemed heavily concentrated in both Miami and Key West.

History would show that the truly big players in Florida were not American - but rather Colombians. I never heard the name Pablo Escobar down in The Keys. Perhaps we were just so small and insignificant that the entire Keys operation amounted to nothing more than pocket lint or a rounding error in the Colombian ledger.

Takeoff the next morning was a joy. With 40 more horsepower and a variable pitch propeller, the Piper's performance put Bluebird to shame. Rocketing upward at 1,500 feet per minute, I was soon on my way to Marathon and the next assignment. One fuel stop and six hours later, I was looking out over Marcos Island and making a beeline for Marathon.

It was an entirely different feeling coming in with a legal airplane. No need for fake N numbers or a concocted story. All the rental paperwork was there, neat and in order should anyone ask. Upon landing, none of the line personnel appeared to recognize me from the week before, but it was Bill Mahoney who signed for fuel that afternoon.

"Have Five-Eight-Tango fueled for an early morning departure," I instructed my Florida counterpart. "I'll be paying cash. And make sure you tie her down properly tonight."

"Yes sir, who's name should we put on the gas ticket?" he asked without understanding the humor behind the question.

"Bill Mahoney," I answered without hesitation.

Shortly thereafter, Vince pulled up in a taxi.

"Really nice to see you again," he said. "I was hoping to god you would actually show up."

"No worries, Vince. I said I'd be back, and here I am. Do we have a plan?"

"Yes, you get your flight plan filed tomorrow, and we take off the following day. One day in Jamaica to get the load arranged, and we fly out the next day. Can that plane handle another 100 pounds?"

"Absolutely," I offered. "It's an awesome airplane. Fast too. We'll cut an hour off the trip."

On the taxi ride back, Vince told me that Alex would not be accompanying us this time to Jamaica. He was on some sort of probation with Johnny, and we would be making a solo trip to the island. Nelson would be our point of contact once in-country. I guess this meant Johnny really trusted that we would come through for him. No babysitter for the trip over and no Alex to escort us once there.

Either that, or they were going to steal the plane and kill both of us at some remote landing strip. The mind never strays far from darker thoughts in this business.

Johnny came to the motel in late afternoon.

"I want to show you the boat," he said. "I don't want any mistakes with the drop."

He drove us to the waterfront where we met Captain Ed, complete with a graying beard, a dirty short-sleeved shirt, tan shorts and no shoes.

"Come aboard," he told us, "but step lively. I've got fishing tackle here and there."

The boat was an almost-new 47' Marine Trader with a huge upper deck and full living quarters down below. The captain gave us a quick tour, including the dual cockpit controls and huge diesel engines.

"Wow," I said impressed, "a fella could live on one of these."

"Yes," he said with a smile. "I do. Now let's get down to business."

Captain Ed took us up to his covered observation deck and made us climb up the narrow ladder.

"See those three reflective stripes running fore and aft?" he demanded. "I'll put some lights on them, and you'll be able to see Mary Belle from miles away. Shield your eyes and let me show you the narrow-beam strobe. I'll be pointing it directly at you. When you see it, turn your landing lights off-and-on three times.

"I have an aircraft radio and will be listening to you on one-eighteen-point-two. When you fly over me, I'll key the mike three times. That's your signal to start the drop. Questions?"

What a relief. Someone who actually knew what they were doing and how to communicate with us.

"What about altitude?" I asked.

"Come in at 3,000 feet, seven miles out on a compass heading of 325°. Start a descent to 1,500 feet and announce to Tower five miles out. That's where I will be laying. Just keep flying straight on that course and I'll follow you in. Kick the groupers out within one minute and we won't have a problem."

"Thank you," I said. "You sound like you know exactly what to do."

"I should. I used to do the drops."

"But not now?" I asked.

"Hell no, too damned dangerous."

Once again, I realized that in the drug world's org chart I fell into the 'expendable' category. Maybe this wasn't such a great career choice after all.

"And by the way," he finished as a sort of compliment, "word's out about you and your encounter with our Customs agent. Great job. You're the youngest guy to ever make a successful run."

As we left Captain Ed, I felt reassured about the professional level of detail for this drop. It was what I had expected out of Alex but never received. Johnny seemed satisfied that everything was in order.

"Thanks Johnny, I feel much better about this deal. It's the level of planning I had anticipated last time around."

"Fucking Alex," he said reflecting on the nature of his cousin, "never was the sharpest tool in the shed. His dad left the scene right before he was born, and his mom's a worthless bitch. My family raised him. We did the best we could with the fucking retard. And now I've become his big brother. He'll be with me until he does something so stupid I can't fix it."

"Like that last stunt?" I inquired gingerly.

"Yeah, that about took the cake. But I've got a damn good line on who's got the pot and where it ended up. I think Axel and Russ played him."

This was my first indication that Johnny might actually be a human being. Previously, I'd thought of him like a vicious shark, endlessly prowling the waters for blood. Maybe that Latin American thing about family being everything was true.

I remembered stories of how the Spanish destroyed their Caribbean realm in the 17th century, bringing inept relatives over, placing them in positions of wealth and advantage, and wondering how the greatest empire of the world could collapse under their feet.

That system of nepotism and elitism, so pervasive even today, seemed to have trapped most of Latin America into a never-ending cycle of despots and strong-men dictators who promise equity but secretly feed their family coffers on the backside. All the while most of their population struggles to get by and pay bribes as a normal course of business.

Johnny dropped us off at the hotel, telling me that Captain Ed had filed a flight plan on my behalf for departure tomorrow morning.

"Wheels up at 8 a.m.," he told me as we stepped out of the Audi. "Don't disappoint me." Looking at Vince he said simply, "you better not fuck this one up."

Neither of us missed the sharp barb pointed in Vince's direction, and we headed into the room to pack our suitcases. I pulled out the maps and realized we would be flying the very same flight profile as last time but with a lot more speed. The Arrow would cut almost 25% off our flight time and should land us in Montego Bay by noon.

129

Vince reached into his pocket. "I really think he believes I had something to do with this," he said as he washed another biscuit down with a quick beer. I'm worried."

"Well, there's nothing we can do but get the second load delivered successfully," I said in an effort to get his mind off the subject. "Come on, let's go take a look at our new ride. That'll make you feel better."

We took off the next morning and made an uneventful flight to Jamaica. The Turbo Arrow was a beautiful machine. With an efficient wing and turbocharged engine, we were able to climb to 13,500 feet, take advantage of the cooler temperature and use the autopilot. Compared to Bluebird, it felt a bit like cheating.

Upon landing, we passed through Customs without a hitch; the officials mostly believed my story that Vince was my copilot. As we left the terminal we were met by the ever-sunny Nelson. He apparently did not have to sleep up a tree and had somehow been made whole by Johnny.

"Oh mahn," he said, "you gotcha a new bird, Five-Eight-Tango."

"*Son of a bitch*," I thought. Five minutes on the island and Nelson already knew the tail number. It made me think that Jimmy had also noted my arrival for another scuba diving trip. Their mutual source must have been somebody in the Customs office or the local FBO.

"Yes," I replied to Nelson as if he understood the technical aspect, "it's a Piper Turbo Arrow IV. Very fast."

"Ah," he said, "no more Bluebird. We gonna call her Sandpiper."

I asked Nelson what he knew about the last drop. I wanted to see if he would offer up some kind of alternative explanation. I was attempting to figure out if he was friend or foe, and if he was driving us off to our doom.

"Yah mahn," he said as we drove off, "I know all about dat deal. Some bad juju for sure."

"It's really none of my business, but may I ask if you were hurt, I mean financially?"

"No man, I jus da middleman here. Johnny got his own connections. I think everything be fine. He got a good name here. He make it right for everybody. No worries, but this one gotta get delivered or my sister she have a cow."

"Your sister?"

"Yah, she married to Johnny's partner here. It all one big family. He hire me to drive you two around all da time. It be all right. No worries."

We drove on in silence for a while. Nelson started to chuckle and began to shake his head back and forth as if to get rid of a bad vision. Then he let out a great big laugh and hit the dash with his right hand.

"Alex a-sleeping in da trees like a monkey," he said. "Now dat's some funny shit. Next time I see him, I gonna drive him right up to a big Banyan tree and tell him, *Mr. Alex, I gotchu a room up on da 4th floor just like you like. I know you be comfortable dare.*"

Nelson kept chuckling to himself before letting us off at the ant motel.

"I come back tonight at eight," he said. "We hear some real music. Special lady in town."

We checked into the same room, its familiar green paint flaking off the wall. I looked for visible signs of the ant army but found no clue. I had stuffed all my clothes in a small backpack and had begun to hang up my shirt in the closet when I noticed something moving on the floor. Turning on the light, I spotted two of the biggest cockroaches I had ever seen scurrying away. I returned my clothes to the backpack.

"What do you think about landing this airplane on the strip?" Vince inquired.

"I don't know. The Piper takes a bit more runway to land. I never calculated the distance last time because the strip isn't on any aeronautical charts. But it looked to be about 2,400 feet long. We should be fine, but I would like to see it tomorrow if Nelson can take us there."

"And if it's not long enough?"

"Well, then we don't make it and all our worries are off."

We headed out down the street to our familiar vendor. "Ah, my friends are back," he said after taking our order.

'For fuck's sake,' I thought, *'is he Nelson's cousin as well, or just a Jamaican offering two tourists a friendly hello?'*

Vince's predicament was beginning to affect me. Every now and then I caught a fleeting glimpse of dread, first dismissing it as nothing and then swatting at it like a gnat buzzing around my face. The fun factor had left, and like a gangrenous wound, paranoia began to circulate around my bloodstream, growing and feeding on itself.

Vince turned to me. "Do you think he remembered us?"

"No Vince," I said. "Stay calm. I'm sure he says that to every tourist who buys off his cart. Don't let your imagination get the best of you."

What I really wanted to say was, *'hand me one of your biscuits, it's getting weird in here.'*

As promised, Nelson picked us up at the motel and headed into what should be generously described as the 'local' part of town. Looking out the passenger window, I noted that both the sky and skin color turned significantly darker the longer we drove.

I like to think I am not prejudiced, but no one's skin shone any whiter than mine[59] as we headed down one side street after another.

A couple minutes later Nelson pulled the car over and we got out, heading into a run-down looking bar whose neon sign once said, *'Trench Town Blues'* but now only said weakly *'rench.'*

---

[59] I have always possessed an amazing internal GPS. Take me to any big city, cut me loose in a car and I can find the worst section of town with uncanny speed; typically ending up on one-way, dead-end streets. Once, I took a series of wrong turns in Los Angeles, eventually Geo-locating myself in Watts during a summer of acute unrest. Heading into a convenience store to ostensibly buy a pack of cigarettes, I sought out the clerk for directions. As she handed me my change and offered directions, she added, "Boy, you sure as hell don't belong here. I suggest you get your ofay ass out of here right now before something bad happens to you."

The place was apparently packed with Nelson's family and friends, and he introduced us over the jukebox din. Of course, it was playing Bob Marley, Jimmy Cliff, Alton Ellis and a host of other reggae musicians, some of whose fame never left the island.

As the houselights dimmed, we found a seat. Hortense Ellis took the stage, wearing a sleeveless sequin dress, with her hair done up in a classy bouffant style high above her slender face. Although I was familiar with Alton, I didn't know about his younger sister. With a backup band, steel drums and three female singers to add harmony, she sang *Unexpected Places* and my heart melted.

Love comes from the most unexpected places
In someone's eyes you never met who wants to get to know you
in someone's smiles you can't forget
and if the music plays on in your mind
take all the love you can find and if love takes you in
Take all the love you can find, and it will come again
...love comes in many ways
in loving arms and sweet bouquets
Nothing said, nothing is ever heard
Here I am outside your door
Trying to tell you just once more
I love you; I really love you

I listened for an hour, pretending to mess with my contacts as tears flowed in the dark hall. I think a deep and abiding truth was born in my soul that night; an understanding that - at the core - we are sound and vibration and frequency.

At break, Nelson took me to the back and introduced me to Hortense. She was autographing her recent *Reflections* album, and I bought a copy. Maybe it was the mix of emotions that struck me so profoundly that night. Paranoia, fear, anxiety, all released - at least for the moment - in the beauty and purity of her voice.

Even today, I can seldom listen to it without tears, remembering the electricity flowing through the crowd that night.

"Not bad," Vince offered in a bit of stupor as we left the club.

"What you think mahn?" Nelson asked as he looked deep into my soul and felt it overflowing.

"Fuuccckkk," was all I could say.

He smiled, squeezed my shoulders with his broad hands and took us back to the motel. It was going to be all right.

"Get some sleep, you two," he said. "Tomorrow morning, we go see the air strip."

––––––––––––

As promised, Nelson showed up around eight the next morning. He had to knock loudly as both Vince and I were sleeping in after some post-concert activities involving the local product. I was going easy on the smoke, in part remembering (or not) that last episode on the beach and needing to keep my pilot skills sharp.

He gave us a few minutes to return to the land of the living and ushered us out the door. Instead of his Toyota Corona, we headed over to an old-school Datsun 510. It resembled nothing as much as a box with wheels but offered a surprising amount of room for 4 adults. It was designed using the same philosophy as the BMW 1600 with a 1.8-liter engine and independent suspension all around.

On the driver's door was a huge white oval with black lettering of the number 42. White racing stripes ran the length of the car, stretching from the hood to the trunk. The rear fender was somewhat bashed in, and a row of huge Hella driving lights adorned the entire front bumper and grill. If I wasn't mistaken, this was a rally car meant for serious off-road competition.

"Dis is Rigley, my cousin. He gonna take us to the airstrip in his Bluebird[60]."

––––––––––––

[60] Datsun sold this car worldwide under various marketing names. In the US it was the Datsun 510. Throughout most of the world, it was marketed as the *Bluebird*. It was nearly indestructible and featured rear-wheel drive; a requirement for the motor sport known as drifting.

Vince and I climbed in, and I presumed we were going back to the air strip used on our last run.

"No, dat one about abandoned," Nelson offered. "You be the first one flew dare in about two years."

Rigley gave us a big Jamaican hello and instructed us to hold on tight. Looking around, I noted there was nothing of substance in the back with which to accomplish his admonition. He fired up the engine and it barked loud. "Ansa exhaust," he said over the ruckus. "And free-flow headers with twin Webbers. She go like scat."

With that we exited the parking lot. Rigley, for the most part, drove sensibly in town but with incessant use of the horn. It wasn't the factory stock '*oh please could you get out of the way*' tone but rather a '*move your ass now*' proclamation.

As we cleared the city and headed down a secondary road, Rigley cut loose with the little beast. We went blasting around the roadway at what seemed like impossibly high speeds and very little body roll. Nelson was able to keep upright, with his left arm clutching Rigley's seat back and his right hand grasping a fat man handle above the passenger door.

Vince and I were not so lucky, bouncing against each other and the side glass. It reminded me of Weebles[61], continually swaying this way and that, occasionally crashing into each other but remaining upright. I could feel a headache coming on.

About 20 minutes into the trip, we left the highway and entered a wide dirt-and-gravel secondary road. Rigley really came into his own, going around corners, kicking the rear end out and 'drifting' through in a graceful, but utterly frightening, arc.

We flew up and down across the terrain, occasionally blasting through roadside businesses and an occasional house here and there. Rigley honked his horn while children and chickens scattered in sincere concern for their well-being. I honestly thought that we might die before getting to the strip.

---

[61] An old Hasbro Playskool toy. "Weebles wobble but they won't fall down."

After about 40 minutes of driving, and by my estimation only 30 miles outside of Montego Bay, we entered a surprisingly flat section of land. This was in stark contrast to the topography of our last landing strip. Rigley turned left and we followed a narrow road for two minutes before stopping at a chained cattle gate.

Getting out of the idling car, whose engine by now was screaming for coolant, Nelson unlocked the gate and swung it open. Ridley eased his Datsun inside the paddock while Nelson secured the gate behind us.

A couple more winding turns through scrubland grass and we reached our destination. Ridley killed the engine, and I said a silent prayer of thanks. I may have squeezed Vince's hand as well.

"Here we are," said Nelson as we piled out of the rally car.

I couldn't quite fathom what I was seeing. In contrast to the last dirt strip, this one was paved with compacted chat, measured at least 75 feet wide and was so long I could not see the end.

"What am I looking at?" I said not comprehending the sheer size of the runway.

"Dis our airstrip," said Nelson proudly.

"My god, how long is it?"

"Oh, 'bout 8,000 feet, more or less."

"Holy shit, you could land a Boeing here."

"What was dat last one?" Nelson asked as he turned to his cousin.

"Seven-twenty-seven," Ridley announced without further comment.

And here, at last, I came to understand the vast nature of the Jamaican drug trade and its inescapable conclusion. The entire country knew about this. The highest rungs in government - at some level - knew this was going on. The military knew this was going on. The locals knew this was going on.

You don't bring a Boeing[62] in at tree top level in rural Jamaica without more than a few people understanding the implications.

It was a vast, vast enterprise. A 727 could conceivably carry up to 50,000 pounds of cargo. Our little Piper Turbo Arrow IV, with a carrying capacity of 400 pounds, was nothing. Or, in our case, everything.

"How does the military not know about this?"

"Of course day do," Nelson said. "We pay dem not to fly their gunship on days when we use the strip."

"You bribe the generals?"

"No, my cousin pay the mechanics and flight crew. Day finds something wrong doing dare inspection. Dem helicopters, day delicate things."

"Is it always the same amount?"

"No, sliding scale. For Sandpiper, $10,000. For mister Boeing, $150,000."

There you have it in a nutshell. A well-oiled machine constantly fed and in need of continuous feeding.

This whole payola scheme aroused my curiosity. "What about the trip Alex arranged on that dirt strip? Who paid the fee?"

"Well," Nelson offered up in a slow confession, "nobody. Alex do it all on the side. Dat why I said you were brave man first time you come in with Bluebird. The Huey was out looking for you dat day. They miss you by about 10 minutes."

I hesitated to ask but did. "What if they had found us?"

"Well, day got guns. Sometimes day like to shoot you down. Looks good for the government to fight the trade now and den."

---

[62]   This might have been the ultimate drug-hauling machine. Freight pilots told me that the triple-engine 727, when free of its cargo, climbed like a fighter and could be rolled like an acrobatic Pitts.

137

Holy mother of god. It really was that close. If I was a violent man, I might be tempted to find Alex and have him whacked. But on second thought, I wouldn't. I have never approved of murder[63], no matter the circumstances.

And it was this goofy sense of honor and propriety that had kept Vince and I alive up to now. I was not going to change philosophical horses in the middle of the stream.

Satisfied that I could in fact land Sandpiper on the ginormous airfield, we departed and headed back to the ant motel.

Ridley, who had shown off his driving skills on the way over, gave us a much gentler ride home.

Tomorrow it was load time.

---

[63] Self-defense is an entirely different matter in my book.

Vince and I knew the routine by now. We cleared Customs, took off to the north, flew 15 minutes and listened for the magic *'radar terminated'* call from the tower.

"All right, here we go again," I said to Vince as we turned off the transponder and dove for the ocean. We leveled out at 200 feet. Sandpiper was so much faster than the Cessna that we got a bit of ground rush flying over the waves. Faster speed also meant less reaction time should we encounter any obstacles[64] on our way back inland.

Ten minutes later we were on final for the runway. It was so massive that it reminded me of flying into a large commercial airport. I was tempted to call both Approach Control and Tower to announce my intentions.

Setting up for landing, I remembered GUMP (Gas, Undercarriage, Mixture, Prop) and brought us in for a smooth touchdown. We back taxied and met Nelson coming out of the bush in a pickup truck. Again, the same routine of carefully dusting each grouper before loading it on the plane. Four hundred pounds as promised.

Nelson supervised the loading, and when finished, came around the plane and gave me a hug.

"You aright, Birdman," he said. "Safe journey home."

I fired up the airplane and took off with 6,000 feet of runway remaining underneath me. Always a good feeling. We headed north and followed the same nap-of-the-earth procedure as before. Once again, I imagined young children waving red and yellow banners at us while we sped by. Another load heading north. Another wheel getting greased. All business as usual.

As I mentioned, nothing enhances the sensation of speed more than flying low to the ground. Vince and I passed over the coast and headed out to open sea a scant 100 feet off the deck. At nearly 170 miles per hour, you could see the swell of five-foot seas for just a split second before they blurred beneath our wing.

---

64   Mostly birds. If you fly into a flock at full speed, one is most assuredly coming through the thin plexiglass windshield. If it hits you in the face, you are most assuredly dead.

139

Unlike the Cessna, whose high wing design allows for an unlimited downward visibility, the Piper with its low wing blocked most of the downward view but allowed for spectacular panorama of the clouds above us.

At some point we would need to climb through and above the inconsequential cloud deck and return to our assigned altitude, but for now we were once again flying in a netherworld, with the ocean below and the clouds above; sandwiching us in a sort of cocoon.

Just as we had done before, I filed a VFR flight plan for the trip. This flight plan, as presented, dictated some specific things. We would fly at an assigned altitude and enter Cuban airspace in a specific window of time. Our entire flight would be about four hours in length and would put us dropping groupers right at sunset. Timing was critical.

"Wow, this reminds me of Star Wars," Vince said as we flew between heaven and earth. "How much farther before we start climbing?"

"About 20 minutes," I replied. "That will put us 60 miles off the coast. We'll get back to our assigned altitude well before Cuban radar picks us up."

At the predetermined time, I pitched the nose up and we began a gentle 500-foot-per-minute climb. If you listen carefully, an airplane will tell you everything you need to know. As the climb begins, the plane slows down a little. As it slows down, the engine has to work harder. As it works harder, the rpm begins to drop.

Sandpiper was equipped with a variable pitch propeller. This feature allowed me to change how much of a bite the propeller took through the air. If you decrease the angle - or bite - it places less strain on the engine and allows the rpm to build back up.

Vince watched me manipulate the controls and asked if he could fly. Although not a pilot, he had been right up front on both trips. I knew he would not do anything stupid.

"Sure," I allowed, "but to start off let's get your feet situated on the rudder pedals. See that ball inside the turn and slip indicator?"

"Yes."

"Okay, gently press forward with your left foot and watch what happens to the ball."

As he did, the plane changed flight dynamics slightly and began to slide, rather than slice, through the air. The ball moved to the right.

"Step on the ball with your foot," I explained. "In other words, put pressure on the right rudder pedal and watch how the ball moves from the right and returns to center. That ball in the center means you are flying the airplane straight and true. That's your job."

Vince kept the airplane flying straight while I gained altitude. He was doing a good job. When we leveled out at 9,500 feet, I trimmed the airplane for straight and level flight.

"Alright, now take the control yoke and keep us at 9,500 feet as shown on the altimeter."

Vince grabbed the yoke and pulled it toward him. We immediately shot up 500 feet.

"Easy there cowboy," I coached. I wanted to say *'think of how a woman only responds to a gentle touch'* but suddenly Megan popped into my head. Get out of there Megan, I'm flying. *'Ride-em-cowboy.'* Shit. *'Harder, harder'.* Shit. Really? Bad metaphor. Bad Megan. Very, very bad Megan. *Wonder where she is now?*

I returned. "Gentle input Vince. Just a light touch. If I've set the controls up properly, the plane really wants to fly itself. Let go of the yoke, or hold it very gently, and see what happens."

Vince relaxed his grip and the plane responded by staying put.

"Now, just a slight forward pressure on the yoke and watch that climb indicator. Oh, and keep your eye on the ball from time to time. You're doing good. Now see the climb indicator start to point negative? Hold it right there for a little while. Two hundred foot per minute descent is about right. Now when we get back down to 9,600 begin to stop your descent and pull back on the yoke."

After a couple of up and down yo-yo rides, Vince got the idea that gentle control input is the key to smooth flying.

"I'm doing it!" he said with excitement. "Look at me! This is super cool."

I was happy to see some worry and paranoia leave his face. We weren't out of the woods by a long shot, but so far, the flight had been flawless. In just about 15 minutes we would call up Cuba, get permission to overfly the country and be on our last leg. Looking at the flight clock, we were right on schedule.

"Good job," I told him. "I've got the controls now. Dial up Cuba Approach."

Vince twisted the appropriate knobs, and we listened as Cuban controllers issued commands to other airborne pilots. They were required by law to speak English, but I had to listen with a careful ear to overcome the heavy Spanish accent.

"Cuba Approach, Piper Five-Eight-Tango with you on one-one-niner-point-five at 9,500; permission to transit Giron."

"Piper Five-Eight-Tango, permission denied."

'What the fuck did I just hear???????'

"Piper Five-Eight-Tango, say again."

"Five-Eight-Tango, Cuba Approach. Permission denied."

'Mother of god.'

"Vince," I asked in utter disbelief, "what did he just say?"

"He said permission denied. What'll we do?"

'Shit, shit, shit. A planeload of pot. Can't fly over Cuba? Can we go back to Jamaica, call their Tower and say just kidding? Fly back at dark and try to find the strip? Fly around Cuba? The airliners do that. Do I have enough fuel? Will Captain Ed still be waiting? Can I hit the deck and buzz Cuba? Do they have Huey's with guns?'

"I don't know Vince. We've flown through here three times now with no problem. Do you think somebody forgot to pay a Cuban bribe?"

"This isn't happening," Vince screamed. "What'll we do?"

Remembering that honesty seemed to work best, I called Cuba Approach and asked directly why permission had been denied.

"VFR flight plans not accepted at this time," came the reply.

I had to think of something, so I pulled this out of my lower extremity. "Five-Eight-Tango, we'd like to amend our flight plan to file IFR[65]."

"Five-Eight-Tango, change approved. Permission to transit."

'Thank you, Jesus, Mary, Joseph, all the saints, guardian angels and anybody else I left out. Amen.'

"Oh my god," said Vince looking at me. "Did that really just happen? Am I dreaming?"

"Yes, it did, and I think I've just used up all my grace points. Let's hope nothing goes wrong from here on out."

We flew on in silence. I seriously contemplated all the bullets I had dodged. I'm not a religious person but I couldn't get past the notion that someone or something was riding shotgun with us. I imagined there was huge accounts due-and-payable line up in heaven with a 'dumb-shits-enter-here' sign and a picture of me hanging over the entrance.

I made up my mind this was the last flight I'd make to Jamaica. Whatever promises I made to Johnny would be squared up when we delivered the groupers.

---

65   Instrument Flight Rules. I did not have an IFR rating at the time and could not legally file such a flight plan. Two months after the trip, the FAA sent out a hearing notice, demanding that I defend myself and show cause for the infraction. I ended up with the only blemish on my flight record, but no fine and no other punishment. I still have that piece of paper.

We crossed over Cuba without incident, flew north for another 60 miles and made a final hard left turn towards home. It was 45 minutes to sunset and 45 minutes to Marathon. We were right on the beam.

"Remember the sequence, Vince?" I asked.

We went over it a couple of times and both felt confident in our ability to find the right boat and drop in a timely manner.

At 10 miles out of Marathon I contacted Tower and advised them of our inbound status. We began our descent down to 3,000 feet on a compass heading of 325°. At eight miles out we were hit with a blinding light from the water. It was Captain Ed!

"I got him," Vince said excitedly. He's right off our nose."

"Great, just keep a visual on his location," I said, toggling the landing lights off-and-on three times in quick succession.

At six miles out Captain Ed lit up the reflective strips on his observation deck. It was perfect. At five miles out we contacted Tower again and listened as the mike clicked three times.

"Drop them Vince" I yelled as he wedged the first grouper in the door and started to kick the packages out in quick succession. Within a minute the load was dropped in a straight line, and we were cleared to land. A flawless execution.

I configured the airplane for final approach. The Piper, like all low-wing aircraft, exhibits 'ground effect' when close to the runway. That is to say the wing creates a sort of air cushion between it and the ground, making for typically smooth landings. This one was a greaser, and we cleared the active runway.

"Five-Eight-Tango, taxi to Customs and hold."

I pulled into the ramp and performed my shut down checklist. As per procedure, Vince and I were required to stay with the airplane while Customs came out for an inspection.

Of course, Customs knew my real name, and I had apparently been flagged in their system as a suspicious character. But because I had flown the flight path flawlessly, they had no probable cause for a search.

144

"You two again?" the stern-faced officer said scanning our cockpit and looking over my documentation.

"Yes sir," I answered.

"Scuba trip?"

"Deep sea fishing, sir."

"I don't know where in the hell you people come from, but I damn sure don't want to see your face around here again. Ever. Is that clear?"

That's funny, I was thinking the same thing.

"Yes sir," I said, and with that we were cleared back into the country.

Vince and I walked into the FBO. I was disappointed to not find a hot chick behind the counter, but rather some nerdish looking goof-head reading Robert Heinlein's *Stranger in A Strange Land*. He looked up at me as if I were interrupting his real job.

"What happened to the hot chick working the counter?" I asked.

"She ran off with some pilot from Ft. Lauderdale."

"So, you're it?"

"Till we get a replacement. What do you want?"

Although we were of similar age, he struck me as a snot-nosed brat. Probably the owner's son. I wanted to give him a lesson in customer service, to instruct him that a proper response ran along the lines of *'good evening sir, how may I help you?'* but he got a few brownie points for reading Heinlein, so I let it pass.

"I've got Five-Eight-Tango over at the Customs ramp. The brakes are set. Please tow it over, top it off and put it in the hangar if you've got space. I'll be in around mid-morning to settle up."

And then, due to the over-polite nature of my Midwest upbringing, I thanked him for his shitty service.

"Just a minute Vince," I said as an afterthought. "I need to use the head."

Walking down the hall, I noted the presence of a fledgling flight school, complete with shirt tails of recent solo students tacked on the wall.

I grabbed a magic marker from the pilot lounge, entered the bathroom and closed the stall door. I drew my now-signature graffiti and signed my name. I figured the snarky kid could clean it off in his spare time.

Bill Mahoney was here

We left the terminal and spotted a black Audi lurking in the shadows. A quick flash of the lights told us it was Johnny. He exited the car as we neared, and I noted that muscle was nowhere to be seen. I took this as a good sign.

He walked up to meet us, and for the first time since meeting him, broke into a wide smile.

"Great job, you two," he said with a slight nod of the head. "I talked to Ed over the radio. We got everything picked up. This will go a long way towards making me whole with Nelson's cousin."

We piled into the car and Johnny took us out for supper. No doubt on the IRS expense account, but who was complaining? About half the bar seemed to know Johnny and kept a respectful distance. One guy came over, shook his hand and left after a brief but secretive conversation.

"The mayor of Key West[66]," he offered. "One of my buddies."

Vince had self-prescribed a biscuit or two and offered one to me. I declined. He wandered off to the dance floor and soon found a partner. Despite his worries, he still maintained a charming exterior around the ladies and was seldom without company.

Johnny and I were left at the table. He leaned in and said, "what about it?"

I knew exactly what he meant.

I exhaled deeply. "I don't think so Johnny, but I appreciate the offer. This business appears to have a lot of moving parts with sharp edges. I think I lucked out a couple of times and I don't want to push it."

"No doubt," he said. "Luck only takes you so far, and in this business, mistakes are not forgiven; they are remembered."

We ordered another round, and I watched, fascinated, as a cavalcade of characters approached Johnny. I presumed the club was his after-hours office and it appeared he was handling a rather full schedule.

"I hear Nelson took you to hear Hortense Ellis the other night," Johnny said during a lull in his tableside business. "Said you were blown away. She had that same effect on me first time I heard her in Kingston. She's got something that reaches deep down into the soul."

Once again, I was impressed with the depth and reach of his knowledge. I wondered if he knew Jimmy back in Montego Bay but realized this was a totally inappropriate question to ask. Those things done in the dark will remain in the dark until the light shines its truth on everything.

He finished his pitch. "There's room for you if you change your mind. You're not bad for a kid. Not half bad at all."

---

66   It was often postulated - but never proven - that certain mayors of certain cities in certain island chains were moving certain products through certain channels outside normal avenues of commerce (and tax collection). These certain individuals appeared to be living way beyond the means that a part-time ceremonial job would normally support.

The next morning Vince and I took a taxi to the FBO. I needed to get Sandpiper back to its owner and Vince was being asked to stay a while longer in The Keys. I didn't want to know any more than I already did about his obligations to Johnny.

As we were looking over the plane, Vince handed me his backpack.

"Here," he said. "It's five pounds. It's all I can do right now."

"Fuck Vince, I'm no dealer. What can I do with this?"

"Sell what you can, and when I get back to the Midwest and get some money coming in, I'll buy it back from you."

I grudgingly accepted his payment, knowing it was all or nothing at this point. I had shot my previous wad on a B&O stereo, and now I owed money for Sandpiper's rental.

Financially, I was about back to square one. So much for dreams, but I was mostly happy to be free of this spider's web and grateful that my friend was still alive. We embraced and promised to meet up in a few weeks' time.

At the FBO, my fellow line service brethren pulled out Sandpiper and parked her in front of the transient lounge.

I walked inside and was relieved to find a smoking hot chick back at the fuel desk.

"Who was running the desk last night?" I asked, remembering the rude young attendant.

"The boss's kid," she said without further comment.

'Ding, ding, ding. Winner, winner chicken dinner,' I thought.

Walking up to the Piper, I admired her sleek lines and the inherent elegance of good design. Form follows function, and there is nothing extra hanging on, no extemporaneous parts, no extra weight.

The only ugly duckling aspect might be the landing gear, and these are merely crutches for a gangling bird, a necessary evil until such time as she breaks free of the earth, tucks them away into little cubby holes, and gets transformed into her true self.

I ran through the Pre-Flight checklist and noted only one small item. It seems a grouper left a minor ding on the passenger side flap. Not enough to warrant corrective action and certainly nothing I would bring up to the aircraft rental facility.

"Clear Prop," I said as I cranked over the engine and waited for Sandpiper to come to life. I love the unique smell of burning av gas[67], and it unleashes not just flying memories but also a remembrance from those skydiving days when we struggled to get outside of the airplane and fall free of its constraints. Hell, maybe we were all just large groupers getting shoved out the door and didn't realize it.

I taxied out towards the active runway, ran up the engine to ensure it was making full power, and received permission to take off towards home.

It was another uneventful flight, with only a slight headwind[68] to slow my progress. I made one fuel stop with a 30-minute break to stretch my legs. Another four hours later, I was on approach to the rental facility.

Per our agreement, I needed to fill up the tanks before handing over the keys.

"How was it?" the manager asked as he tallied up the final charges.

"It's a beautiful airplane," I said. "The autopilot worked flawlessly, and I got the fuel burn down to 10 gallons per hour on lean cruise. What more could I ask for?"

---

[67]   Unless it is coming out of my car's tailpipe.

[68]   Headwinds can be a real issue. Sometimes these winds will blow up to 60 miles an hour. Do the math. The plane flies at 120 mph but meets a headwind of 60 mph. 120 - 60 = 60 miles per hour of actual ground speed. On days like that, you can look out the window and watch cars on the highway outpace you. Not an inspiring feeling.

"We appreciate your business," he said handing me the bill. Our initial estimates of rental charges had been very accurate, and the money order I gave him prior to departure covered the bill.

Reaching into the cash register, he handed me $27.34 in change. "Thanks for your business," he said. "Next time you come back we might have something even faster."

I looked at the money. Probably enough to get a fucking happy meal at McDonald's and fill up the MGB. What a world, but at least I was free of the Key West crowd. That counted for a great deal.

I walked into the sunlight with a backpack full of high-grade pot and no real customer base.

I needed to start making some new friends. A lot of them.

A Door-to-Door Salesman

In 1959, Jay Van Andel and Richard DeVos got tired of ice fishing in Michigan and started a business called Amway (American Way) selling health, beauty and home care products. Through the decades it has done very, very, very well. In 2019 the company booked revenues in excess of $8.7 billion.

Richard's daughter-in-law Betsy DeVos was appointed Secretary of Education by former President Trump in 2017. Her father is a billionaire, and her brother founded a mercenary company first known as Blackwater USA. She is my age and makes me realize what a phenomenal underachiever I have been throughout life.

Amway uses a Multi-Level Marketing platform to sell their products. The Federal government has another name for this structure. They call it a pyramid scheme, yet have remained unsuccessful in proving this claim in any number of court cases over the decades.

Multi-Level Marketing structures are known as pyramids because they rely on continually recruiting new people and their money into the base (or pyramid) of the organization. The more people you recruit, the higher up you go in the pyramid. The higher up you go, the more money you get as a sort of tribute from everyone brought in under your wing. At the very top, early adopters got a sort of kickback from everyone who joins. Some of them are multi-millionaires.

This setup proved wildly attractive to many of my relatives, and it seemed like everyone I knew had a sister or uncle who sold Amway. The company's initial product was called LOC (Liquid Organic Cleaner), and it came in a blue plastic bottle. I suppose it worked fine, but the pressure to purchase was always intense and off-putting to me.

While it was acceptable to slam the door on a Jehovah's Witness, your uncle was a harder nut to crack. In such a manner, most Amway distributors wedged their toes into every door they could find.

When growing up, you were likely to walk into a neighbor's house and spot a gaudy blue Amway bottle on the countertop, almost always unused. It was a sure sign they had likewise been guilted into a purchase.

That was me with product to move. Like an Amway distributor, I was merciless and desperate, wedging my foot into every door with a visible crack.

I would call up friends and attempt to compel them to purchase one ounce. Most of them were poor[69], and we would dicker down the amount until I walked away with $20 in my pocket. It was going to be a long haul to get rid of 5 pounds when selling it 1/4 ounce at a time.

I'd call on old skydiving buddies that I had not talked to for a few years. After pleasantries, I would make my pitch. "Are you in the business now?" they would ask. I'd hit up everybody I knew at college, peddling my wares and asking for referrals.

I burnt up the road in my MGB, going from town to town like a common door-to-door salesman out of the 1950s. And in the ultimate sort of desperation, I converted a crush-proof Halliburton Zero aluminum photography suitcase into a traveling display case.

I plied the roads for six weeks, looking for a buyer here and there. In the meantime, I went back to work part time, delivering pizzas. My, how the mighty had fallen.

The real issue of course was not finding a willing buyer. Almost everyone I knew back then was smoking now and again. The problem was that I was bucking up against an already-established distribution network like the one Johnny had in place.

---

[69] Years and years later I reunited with a photographer friend. We were reminiscing on old times, and out of the blue he said, "I only have one regret with our friendship." I prepared myself for a heavy emotional blow and he confessed, "I wish I had bought more of that Jamaican pot you were selling. That was the best stuff I ever smoked."

He sat at the top of his organization, and had perhaps five people like Vince underneath him. When my load arrived, each of these department heads[70] would take 60 pounds. Each department head would in turn further distribute their portion to six managers. These managers, with 10 pounds in their hands, would go to five section heads and distribute 2 pounds each. Finally at the street level, worker bees would sell the pot one ounce at a time to already established buyers.

No one was buying from an independent agent.

At the same time, I had been keeping tabs on Vince through a mutual acquaintance. He had come back from The Keys and was under intense pressure to make up for Johnny's lost revenue. Vince was, according to friends, starting to drink non-stop, popping quaaludes daily and becoming increasingly paranoid. He was convinced that Johnny was going to kill him.

I caught a lucky break and contacted an old friend in Houston. He had a friend who had a friend who might be willing to buy 3 pounds from me, but at a deeply discounted price. I did what any door-to-door salesman would do and hopped in the car with my Halliburton Zero in the trunk.

But somewhere in Oklahoma a deep foreboding came over me. I had kept my phone off the hook for fear that some of the Key West gang would contact me. I wanted nothing to do with them, and yet the idea that I was somehow still obliged got under my skin.

Being a good salesman, I had started smoking some of my pot by then; strictly to offer personal testimony about its efficacy. Well, maybe more than a few samples. This no doubt contributed to my growing fears.

Paranoia's grip is sneaky and insidious. It feeds from the inside and springs up fully grown without much warning. The only thing I can compare it to was a deep depression I entered into once in my life. It was so dark that I thought killing myself was the only way out.

---

[70] If you think this sounds like Amway, a modern business structure or even the Catholic church, you would be right on the money. Hierarchical organizations all operate the same, regardless of the product they are selling.

When my paranoia finally hit home, it arrived in full force. I was convinced each four-door Ford I met in oncoming traffic was an undercover agent, tracking my every move. In desperation, I found a country road in the middle of Oklahoma and stashed the Halliburton in a hedge row.

I drove for 30 minutes, waiting for police who never came to pull me over. *'Like a dusted off grouper,'* I thought, *'they won't find a trace in my car.'*

After a while, I came down off the edge and turned around. No one was following me. No one knew I had a trunk full of pot. There were a million Fords on the road and not one of them was tracking me.

It's safe to say that one country road in Oklahoma looks much like every other. It took a good hour to locate the Halliburton and continue my trek southward.

In Houston, my friend came through. His contact purchased three pounds, but not for $3,000. I drove back to the Midwest with $1,500 in hand and an exhausted countenance.

I headed back to my apartment and switched on the B&O. Traffic[71] seemed appropriate and I listened as Capaldi and crew sang:

'Your old man's headed for the final payoff
the joker that you have is fading too
and all the sharks that come around for the rip off
are going to tear the flesh right off you'

I couldn't shake the feeling that the sharks were coming up from Florida. I went out and bought a .38 Special, waiting for the inevitable.

And then it happened. Vince finally reached me on the phone.

"Johnny is on his way," he said in full panic. "And he's bringing that guy with him."

That's when my deepest fears materialized. There was blood in the water and the sharks were circling.

---

[71]   Traffic. *Walking In the Wind* from their album *When The Eagle Flies*

It All Falls Apart

I agreed to meet Vince at a mutual friend's house, seventy miles removed from my apartment. I wanted to keep as much distance as possible from the train wreck.

It was hard to fathom just how far this story had strayed from its original vision. From easy money and owning my own airplane to scrounging for a dollar and hiding from the death squad, it was all spinning out of control.

"What am I going to do?" a greatly diminished Vince asked me when I arrived. "Johnny is coming up with muscle this weekend."

"What do they want?"

"Fifty thousand dollars," he said in exasperation. "I've got $15,000 right now and Mike owes me $25,000. He keeps saying he'll pay me, but I don't know that it will be enough."

"Has Johnny threatened you?" I asked Vince.

"He said he was going to fucking kill me if I didn't have the money. I think he means it this time. And he said he wants to see you."

"I'm out Vince," I said evenly. "I did what I promised, but there is no way I'm getting involved again. None of this has turned out like you said it would. It's all a nightmare. And when Johnny shows up, I will not be around."

I had in my mind another squeeze play, where Johnny would require me to fly again in return for sparing Vince. I was not going to put myself in that situation a second time.

"What about the rest of my pot? Are you able to buy it back and help me out?"

"No, I'm sorry," he said. "I need to keep every dollar that comes in for now."

I understood his predicament. I hoped that Vince understood mine.

"I'm out of here Vince," I said. "Good luck. I won't be picking up the phone."

With that, I walked away and watched from afar as storm clouds exploded on the horizon.

———————

Johnny and muscle showed up that weekend at Eli's house and had a long talk with Vince. I don't what was said, but he remained alive.
Our mutual friend called the following Tuesday with an update.

"You have no idea how scared I was," Eli replied. "That Johnny is pure evil. He came into my house and insisted we put him up for the weekend. His sidekick is scary as fuck. Cindy and I left the house for most of the weekend. I thought we were going to come back to a murder scene. I really did."

"Where's Vince?"

"He went out to find Mike. I guess Mike owes Vince something like $20,000 and Vince promised Johnny he'd have it in a week."

"What happened to Johnny?" I asked.

"They left Sunday night and drove back to Florida. He kept asking about you."

"I knew he would. I think he wants me to fly again."

"Will you?"

"No. I'm out forever with this shit. I'm going to stick to flying skydivers at the DZ."

Eli and I had met at the university some years back and became good friends. He was Jewish, and for some reason, he and his friends let me into their close-knit circle. A cynical view was that I became their token goyim, but I think it went way beyond that for us.

He was one of the few people who took me up on the challenge to make a first jump. In the following two years, he and I jumped together often. To the chagrin of his father, Eli dropped out of school for a while and became a genuine 'jump bum.' That's the real tribe membership in my book.

"Why the hell did you introduce Vince to me?" Eli asked.

"Ah, pardon me, but it was the other way around in the dorm, remember?"

"Oh yeah, but in my book, he is still your friend."

"Is there anything I can do on this end to help?" I asked with genuine concern.

"I don't know. Just get Vince the fuck out of our lives. This is some scary shit." And as an afterthought he said, "but dude, flying out of Jamaica. That's unreal. I want to hear all about it when this is over."

I hung up and went into the back room to count my product. I was down to 2 pounds, minus the quality control checks I kept performing. It was without a doubt the best pot I ever smoked, although I don't know how it would stack up against today's legal varieties.

A few days later the phone rang. It was my Houston friend.

"Wow, that's apparently some pot," he said. "My buddy wants to buy some more. Can you sell him another couple pounds?"

Sensing a business opportunity and thinking like an Amway salesman, I told him I only had one pound left and the price was $2,500.

"Hold on, let me ask him," he said putting the phone down. A minute later he rejoined the conversation. "It's a deal, when can you come down?"

"I can't, I'm holed up for a while."

And then, in perhaps the stupidest moment of the entire escapade, I offered up this: "How about I FedEx it to you?"

"Sure, why not?" he replied, and he gave me his address.

Next afternoon the doorbell rang. I looked through the peep hole to find a FedEx man, prepaid box in his hand.

"Come on in," I said taking the box from his hand. "I'll just be a minute."

Running to the bedroom, I shut the door and tried desperately to stuff one pound into the box. I had triple and quadruple wrapped my product in multiple baggies and convinced myself it didn't smell. Much. Well, not that much.

"Here you go," I said offering him the bulging package. He gave me a tracking number and promised next day delivery. I called my buddy in Houston and told him to expect it next day.

When it failed to arrive, I called the FedEx Hot line and gave them my tracking number. I got transferred about three times before reaching Gloria in Memphis. The conversation in pure southern dialect went something like this:

'Miiissstterr Enright, this is Glloorriiaa at the FedEx facility here en Memmpphiss. Youurrr paacckkage broke open las night on the convauh belt and waass found to contain drruuggs."

Being the over-polite Midwesterner, I thanked her for the information and hung up.

Mother of god. Where does this lead? How soon before the cops show up? Do I hit the street now or confess my crimes and give up? The paranoia was growing, and now for good reason.

––––––––

In the meantime, Vince's grace period with Johnny was up. I knew Vince was out looking for Mike, desperately seeking the $25,000, now in arrears for over a month.

Wow, time to keep up with my quality control protocol and smoke a bowl.

Three days later, the phone rang. It was Eli.

"Have you seen the newspaper?" he asked in a panic. "Mike is dead. I think Vince killed him."

Not being local, I drove 40 miles into town and picked up the local rag.

There, above the fold on page one, was a developing story. Local man shot and killed late in the evening. Further details as they become available. Police think drugs may have been involved.

"My god," I called back to Eli. "Why do you think it was Vince?"

"It's my best guess. Who else would it be? And now, no one can get hold of him. He seems to have disappeared."

Over the next week more details emerged. The headlines read like every other crime novel:

- Police Have leads
- Hot Line Established
- Drugs Suspected, Possible Florida Connection
- More Information Sought
- Investigation Continues

My fear was overpowering. I wondered why the police had not yet shown up to arrest me. I convinced myself that a surveillance crew had been set up across the street[72] to monitor me. Just because you are paranoid doesn't mean they are not out to get you.

Twice now, honesty had saved me. I decided it was time to talk to the police. But I wanted a little insurance beforehand. I found an electronics store and purchased a micro cassette recorder. If I was going to talk to the cops, I wanted to record the conversation.

---

[72] I really think a surveillance crew had been set up. I got out a pair of binoculars one afternoon and watched them looking hard in my direction. When they spotted me, I waved. Suddenly their curtain was drawn.

It took one day for the detectives to arrive. My downstairs neighbor, admirer of my stereo, noted their presence and asked me later who they were. I lied.

Before I let them in, I duct taped the recorder underneath my kitchen table and pressed 'record.'

A cop's first question is always along the lines of 'why are you coming forward?'

In truth it was threefold: a bargaining chip in case I was under surveillance, a back stop of protection from Johnny, and a moral revulsion against the killing.

"I don't sanction murder," I told them plainly.

We spent about 19 minutes and 30 seconds talking before a loud thunk interrupted our interview.

"What was that?" the detective asked, knowing full well the sound of a recorder shutting off.

"Might be a recorder," I offered sheepishly.

"For what purpose?"

"To make sure my interests are protected, and that this conversation is preserved."

"Well, why don't you just bring it out and put it on the table?"

I extracted the recorder from underneath the table, removed the duct tape, flipped the tape over and hit the record button for a second time.

I told them of my involvement as a pilot but did not give up names or offer thoughts about who might have killed Mike. I mentioned my fear of Johnny and told them I had purchased a gun for self-protection.

"What kind?"

".38 Special," I replied, and all their ears perked up.

"Can we see it?"

One of the cops unholstered his weapon and the room grew tense. This is where people die. I've seen it in the movies.

"Bring it out unloaded," he added as an afterthought.

I went into the bedroom and brought the gun out; brand new and still in its box. It was unloaded and had never been fired.

The detective put on a pair of gloves and examined the chamber. Saying nothing, he handed it back to me.

"Thanks for your cooperation," he finished. "We'll be in touch."

With that, the trio left.

———————

I had crossed some kind of threshold by cooperating with the police. It certainly put me at odds with Johnny and his crew. But the local police were not interested in Key West happenings. They wanted to know who killed Mike. In reality, they probably wanted to pin a medal on the killer for removing a low-life drug dealer from their streets.

After three more key interviews were obtained, the police announced that Vince was now wanted in connection with the murder. He was to be considered armed and dangerous, a fugitive from the law.

While I suspected that Vince had murdered Mike, it did not square with the fun and congenial soul that I had spent time with and knew deeply.

I knew that in some way, the Key West crowd had maneuvered Vince into a dark corner, pressuring him to make good on a lost load whose true architect was Alex. At some point - and aided heavily by incessant drug use - he snapped.

To add one more component to the surreal nature of the time, the police entered my apartment without a warrant and took my gun for testing.

"Those men who came by to see you the other day were back," my neighbor said. "They went into your place when you were not home."

161

I found this almost impossible to believe. Police would not break into my apartment and search it without a warrant.[73] I've seen all the shows, I know how it works. I thanked her for the information and filed it under the 'not true' section of my brain.

The police had no further contact with me, and I continued to scan the newspaper for daily updates. About three weeks after the indictment, Vince turned himself in, confessed to the murder, waived a trial and was quickly sentenced to a state penitentiary.

Somewhere in the vast rice fields of Louisiana, Vince told me later, the heavens had opened and revealed the Son of God to him. He fell on his face, was born again and turned himself in. That was his story.

"That's fucking bullshit," said one of Eli's Jewish friends as we talked after the sentencing. "Vince doesn't get a pass just by mouthing someone's name. He killed my friend Mike, and he deserves to pay."

"An eye for an eye?" I inquired.

"Damn right. I hope he gets reamed every night in prison. Even that wouldn't be enough. Nothing will bring Mike back."

And here my Jewish friends and I came upon a great theological chasm, never bridged even to this day. Despite parallels in their Torah about lambs without spot or blemish atoning for their collective guilt, they could not understand the Christian notion of Jesus' sacrifice covering and forgiving every sin.

---

[73] Three months later I decided the terror was over. I returned my gun and asked for a full refund. "It's a used gun," said the dealer, "but I'll buy it back." When I told him I had never fired the gun and showed him the box of bullets, he opened the chamber and showed me powder burns.

Mike had been shot five times with a .38 Special. The police had taken my gun and apparently test-fired it to see if it was a ballistics match. Satisfied that it was not, they returned it in secret. Believe this or not.

162

Perhaps modern Jews are too far removed from practicing actual blood sacrifices on the altar to find any parallels, and no amount of pot or beer brought us any closer to a shared understanding.

I don't offer Vince's conversion as a free pass on murder, but simply as an observation from that time.

———————

I let a year pass before going to see Vince.

The FBO had changed ownership, and no one was talking about a missing airplane. FedEx was apparently not interested in me, Johnny had faded away back to The Keys, and I had returned to the DZ, flying skydivers and jumping from time to time.

Every time I brought the Cessna 182 in low over the trees and set up for landing on the short grass strip, images of Jamaica would fire off in my frontal lobe. When we were on jump run and the hinged door swung open, I thought about Vince kicking groupers out of Bluebird and Sandpiper.

My skydiving friends knew most of the details, and in their eyes, I gained a measure of fame. One Vietnam vet even gave me his aviator wings to wear on my leather coat. He said it was to honor my courage and not my wisdom.

———————

Over conversation one evening with Sherry, a girl from my hometown, I learned her brother Fred was in the same prison as Vince.

Like me, Fred had some run ins with the law. Unlike me, he kept at it and was eventually sent away to the big house. I told Sherry I would like to accompany her to prison to see both Vince and Fred.

Vince knew I was coming and looked forward to the visit. I was the only one of his friends willing to come see him, and he was anxious to tell me about his conversion experience. We had shared a brief but intense time together, and those bonds were not easily broken.

As we passed through the prison gates and into the visitor complex, I was struck with a deep sense of dread. This place would be my hell. Dark walls, violence, complete authoritarian controls, no freedom of movement. The smell. I shook my head and thanked God for an almost unbelievable amount of grace and protection that allowed me to both walk in and walk out of this purgatory at will.

Vince was exuberant, and back to his old self, but with a new perspective on everything. I know the evangelical mindset and walked in it for a long time. Its language is not off-putting to me, and Vince was basking in it.

"I'm free!" he said to me.

"I don't know," I replied looking around at the prison. "Looks to me like you are going to be here for a long time."

"No, I mean I'm free inside. Whom the Son hath set free is free indeed!"

We talked God for 15 minutes in a way that none of my Jewish friends could comprehend. Vince had a long time to redeem himself, and only time would tell if his conversion experience would be deep and lasting, or fade away with time.

Sherry sat next to me and listened to Vince's story. As her brother entered through a side door, her eyes brightened. I followed her glance and saw Fred moving towards our table.

As he neared, Fred cast a harsh glance at me, perhaps wondering who Sherry had brought into his small and confined world. As he looked closer, a broad smile of recognition came over him. He realized it was a familiar face from his old hometown.

He yelled my name from halfway across the room, and I gave him a wave as Vince watched the exchange in disbelief. Fred ran up to Sherry, gave her a big hug and pumped my hand in glad recognition. Vince shook his head and laughed, something I had not heard for a long time.

"Unbelievable," Vince said as I made introductions. "You really do know everybody. Even in here. What are the odds?"

"Apparently 100%," I shot back.

Epilogue – 2024

Seeing Vince behind bars brought a sharp focus to my insanity. The promised easy money had evaporated, replaced by a harsher phrase of ten-to-life. The stupor of the times was wearing off both collectively and individually. I locked Bill deep in the recess of my past, to be visited only occasionally with close friends or when a flash of memory would flare up.

Aviation had worked itself into my bloodstream and could not be easily flushed out. I looked at the major career paths of either flying airplanes or repairing them. Although I retain a keen interest in the mechanical side of things, I chose the flying route.

I eventually finished my degree and put it in my back pocket. It's a calling card but, until recently, not a requirement to fly professionally. I started to take flying seriously, accumulating the required ratings of Commercial, Instrument, Multi-Engine and Certified Flight Instructor.

Following the path of almost every professional pilot, I instructed students, building flight time in my logbook while in pursuit of the next job. I flew bank checks in a beat-up Aero Commander, sometimes flying down to minimums without benefit of an autopilot, looking desperately for clouds to clear as I approached hidden runways.

I learned to fly seaplanes. I took a check ride for my ATP rating, the real gateway into professional aviation. I spent hundreds of hours in Beechcraft Bonanzas, turbine singles and eventually their top-of-the-line Super King Air.

I built two airplanes, one entirely made of wood and the other almost entirely of modern fiberglass and resin. I got my tail wheel endorsement, allowing me to fly a variety of older airplanes. I even owned a Pitts for a while, doing aerobatics in the sky and thinking about Fast Eddy flying inverted over wheat fields and collecting stains on the top of rudder.

Unlike many pilots, I did not aspire to fly for the commercial airlines. I had no interest in driving buses around the sky all day despite the pay and benefits.

Instead, I chose the private sector of General Aviation with endless opportunities stretching every which way. There was a whole world of small aircraft you could dive into. A world of freight hauling, a world of manufacturing, a world of business jets and of corporate flight departments. A world designing radio and navigation equipment, a world of selling pilot supplies, a world of restoring vintage aircraft.

After ten years of paying my dues and accumulating 5,000 hours of flight time, I made my way into the business jet world. Perhaps this was returning to my first love, thinking about the early days of towing and fueling those machines.

Even within this world, there was a great stratification. At the top end of the spectrum were planes like the Gulfstream Model 700, costing $80 million, flying up to 7,000 miles without refueling and weighing more than some commercial airplanes.

At the other end were baby jets, costing $4 million, flown by owner-operators and carrying 5 people for 1,000 miles. My career landed me somewhere in between these extremes, flying new business jets that typically cost between $10 million and $20 million each.

The finest people I ever knew lived inside this world. Many of these jets were purchased by owner/operators, a breed of pilots who were successful enough in business to spend $4 million (and up) on a single purchase.

Almost to a man[74] these entrepreneurs had grown their business along with their flying skills and interests. It was a chicken-or-egg kind of thing. Did the airplane help expand their business, or did they grow their business to support their airplane habit? In almost all cases it was impossible to divide the two.

The typical owner/operator started out with a small business and a Cessna 172. As the business grew, the airplane became a tool, helping to expand their territory. As the territory grew, they needed an airplane with longer range. This symbiotic relationship kept growing, bootstrapping itself until finally a company worth $40 million could justify the purchase of a business jet.

---

[74] If it sounds like this was a man's world, it was. I don't pretend to know why this was or offer a critical theory on exclusion. It was just the lay of the land, but from my perspective the world was open to whomever was drawn into it.

The owners who walked through our front doors were certainly millionaires, but with few exceptions had none of those stereotypes portrayed on TV. They were super smart businessmen who loved aviation. And I loved being around them.

Aviation was our passion, and I never understood why someone would spend their life's energy doing something in which they had no real connection.

"You know what I hate about this city?" a coworker once asked. "Every time you look up you see an airplane."

"You know what I love about this city?" I replied. "Every time you look up you see an airplane."

Yet this passion, this beautiful obsession if you will, came at a cost. I buried a few friends due to chemical poisoning that was finally acknowledged by the industry. We laid to rest a professional pilot when water contaminated his fuel system and caused him to crash at takeoff. I watched marriages crumble and was myself twice a victim of what we in the industry cynically referred to as AIDS[75].

I wrote technical manuals and dabbled in CATIA drawings. I lived and worked among engineers for many years and rewrote factory procedures in never-ending challenges to increase plant efficiency.

But of all the jobs I held within that giant behemoth of a factory, the most memorable was serving as a liaison between the factory and our customers. At times there was a three year wait to buy a new airplane, and customer contact was limited. At other times the order book got skinny, and it was a fast-and-furious process between contract signing and delivery.

In the last month before delivery, it was always some sort of controlled chaos and putting out fires, all in anticipation of the Delivery Day. It was in this liaison role, helping to deliver new airplanes, that I coined a phase destined to find its way outside our walls.

---

[75] **A**viation **I**nduced **D**ivorce **S**yndrome

Every Thursday, the company would hold a coordination meeting between Manufacturing and Delivery. The status of each airplane's build process and delivery date to the customer would be discussed. Inevitably manufacturing would miss their promised delivery dates, causing no small amount of angst on the customer end.

One week you would go to the meeting, and the manufacturing team would say the airplane was 'on schedule' for delivery next Friday. We would call the customer and give them the good news. They would make travel arrangements to pick up their new airplane, often bringing an entire team in for delivery.

The next Thursday as the customer was flying in - often from overseas - the manufacturing team would announce that the airplane delivery had slid three weeks and a new schedule had been put in place. "It's on schedule to the new schedule" they would say with a straight face.

"It's time for the Liar's Club," I said one Thursday in anticipation of their chronic and frustrating delays. "Let's see what Rolodex excuse they pull out today." Somehow this phrase slipped out of my inner circle and into wider circulation. Delivery meetings became almost universally known as the Liar's Club.

These frequent delays caused internal chaos as well. In preparation of delivery, we would order elaborate catered lunches requiring a day's notice to prepare. When the airplane and customers failed to materialize in the delivery hanger, we were left with platters of exquisite food.

Rather than let these meals go to waste, we would call each other on the phone using secret code.

"Climb Mount Niitaka[76] in Delivery Room B" meant another delivery had fallen through and food was there for the taking. Like ants in Jamaica, there would be a steady stream of people sneaking up the back stairs and getting lunch courtesy of the company.

Management often accused us of creating false delivery dates to get a free lunch. The reality was that the organization was shooting itself in the foot, failing to communicate realistic and transparent delivery dates during the Liar's Club.

---

[76]   Code phrase used by the Japanese on December 7, 1941, to announce the Pearl Harbor invasion was on.

"I'm not surprised we keep shooting ourselves in the foot," a chief inspector once told me as he surveyed the scene, waiting for a plane that failed to arrive. "What does surprise me is the rapidity at which we reload."

For almost a quarter of a century I worked in the business, accumulating friends and business acquaintances throughout the world. As a pilot and licensed mechanic, I got a sort of pass into many back-shop areas of Flight Departments and manufacturers. It's a bit of a secret club, maybe like the Masons in which a certain signal lets you into the inner sanctum.

When I retired last year, I moved back to Florida and bought an old Cessna 172. It's not a fast airplane but it is honest and forgiving. And despite my ego, there are certain motor skills that begin to diminish with age. The Cessna is slow, and I am right in line with it. It suits me well and I spend my days flying from small airport to small airport in search of hamburgers.

Always, and for eternity to come, is the FBO. It's the gas station, the 7/11 found at every airport in some form or another. And it was here, two months ago, that I found Bill Mahoney, apparently alive and well in the middle of the state.

I had not planned on stopping at this small airport, but Florida weather arrives without much notice. The squall line showed up on radar and prudence found me landing at a smaller field with no control tower.

Leaving the active runway, I spotted the only FBO on the field and headed towards it. A lone lineman saw me coming in and waved me to a stop. I completed my shutdown checklist and told him to add 15 gallons a side.

"Got a bathroom?" I asked.

"Yes, inside the door, past the pilot lounge and down the hall to your right."

I stepped inside and surveyed the familiar scene, almost a replica layout of every FBO in every small airport. The front desk was empty. Apparently, the lineman was doing dual duty pumping gas and running the register.

I poked my head inside the pilot lounge, noting a few shirttails pinned on the wall that displayed recent solo dates. It looked to be a small but active flight training department. I knew that somewhere out in the pattern was an instructor trying to act calm while a student pilot did their best to kill them both.

I made my way back to the dingy bathroom. It appeared to be seldom cleaned by the line crew. As I shut the stall door and set down to examine the local graffiti, I nearly fell off my seat. Somebody had sketched Bill Mahoney on the door.

Bill Mahoney was here

I could not believe my eyes. I really couldn't. I sat there for a minute and looked at Bill peaking over the wall at me, his beady eyes lighting up a memory I had not considered for decades.

Attempting to get up, my world started to tilt. I grabbed at the ADA bars on both sides of the stall, looking for support. A slight buzzing noise entered from the back of my head and moved counterclockwise twice around my brain. It was replaced by a loud pop centered between and above my eyes. The world went dark, and I fell back into time.

"Sir, are you okay?" the lineman asked as he rapped on the door.

I shifted out of some other place, and from thence, back to the present. "Yes, thanks for checking. I'll be out in a minute."

I took a deep breath and opened the door. I was physically shaking and in no shape to fly. *Was this a heart attack? What in god's name just happened in there?*

"I'd like to use the pilot lounge and lay down for a while," I said as I emerged.

"No problem," he said. "Do you want me to tie down Bluebird?"

"Excuse me?"

"I said do you want me to tie down your airplane? There's a front moving in later this afternoon."

"Please," I responded. "I think I'm done flying for the day."

Walking into the pilot lounge, I was hit again with a flood of memories. These lounges are universally tired and worn out, but serve as an inner sanctum, a holy of holies[77] for pilots. There is a universal brotherhood inside the door, and non-pilots avoid the lounge like there was some sort of repulsive magnetic force that makes them want to walk on by.

For pilots, it's home. It's the cave. It has historically been a boy's club, yet women are welcome as well. It's not about XX vs. XY, but rather more of an understanding that the brotherhood of the initiated makes no such distinction.

I walked over to the EZ-Boy and sat down, moving the lever to the fully reclined position.

EZ-Boy? *'Easy there cowboy'* came flooding back into my consciousness as I tried to remember what triggered that phrase and where it came from.

I closed my eyes and moved completely out of time.

An hour later I woke up, fatigued and unrested. Something had happened. Something in my world had shifted. I felt like my gyros had tumbled and I was falling out of a cloud.

---

[77] In the Old Testament, the temple at Jerusalem had several outer and inner courts. At the very center was the Holy of Holies, the place where God's presence and the Ark of the Covenant dwelt. According to the story, it was such a powerfully pure place that priests entered with a rope attached around their waist. If they were impure, the presence of God would illuminate them and strike them down. The attendants would pull on the rope and haul the deceased out of the inner sanctum. Not a place for the impure, the uninitiated or for posers.

"Can I borrow the airport car for the night?" I asked.

"Old-timer, aren't you?" he offered without judgment. "We got rid of those beaters some years back, but I can call an Uber for you. Where do you want to go?"

"Got any discounted hotels?"

'Yep, pilots get a discount down at The Hampton. Want me to set it up?"

I waited while he made arrangements for me. I have a smart phone but still prefer the intimacy of a human voice. And I missed the smoking hot chicks at the front desk. We chatted while waiting for the Uber to show up.

I asked him about the graffiti in the bathroom.

"That Bill Mahoney thing? I have no idea where it started, but it's apparently everywhere in these old FBOs. Pilots tell me they see it all over the country. My boss made me repaint the stall a couple of times, but as soon as we got it repainted, some flyer would come in, buy gas, and redraw him. We finally gave up. Who is Bill Mahoney, anyway?"

I let the question remain unanswered and pursued another line of inquiry.

"Are you a pilot?" I asked him.

"Working on it," he said, and his world came alive. "I soloed last month. That's my shirttail in the lounge."

"Cool. How's it going?"

"I'm having a little trouble understanding VORs," he offered. "I don't know why they still use those things. I've got GPS."

"Don't worry, it'll come," I offered as encouragement. "And don't forget to put your head on a swivel and look outside the cockpit from time to time. The GPS will get you lost. You need a map. And by the way, your real compass is internal."

The Uber pulled up and I sped away towards The Hampton.

"Can you stop at a liquor store?" I asked the driver. "I want to get a beer."

Of course, ABC Discount Liquor did not have a Red Stripe. I settled for Yuengling, the unofficial beer of Florida. At least in my Florida. In the hotel, I plugged in my smart phone and watched a classic movie on TCM before falling asleep.

The next morning, I felt refreshed and mostly back in my own world. Taking an Uber back to the FBO, I was greeted at the front desk by an older blond. She was 60, trim and still hot in my book.

"Worked here long," I asked?

"Thirty-five years," she said with a smile. "I guess it's been my whole life."

"Seen some shit, haven't you?"

"Oh, you have no idea," she said and lit up like a firefly.

"I might have some idea," I shot back as a small electrical current passed between us.

"Have you been topped off?" inquired the imp.

I just smiled. "Last night, but thanks."

"Have a safe flight," she offered as I walked out the door and headed to my blue-striped Cessna.

And that benediction, offered by her perhaps a thousand times, went straight up to heaven and into the arms of Mary and Jesus; and from thence into the throne room of God where her request was granted.

At home during the following week, memories came flooding back in an astounding rush. It was all I could do to try and keep up with impressions that kept exploding like a Fourth of July nighttime display.

If I was still in the drug world, I would say that I'd swallowed enough mushrooms to watch electricity flow through the walls. But this was not drug induced and not a trip. These were synapses firing off in my brain.

Maybe that *'clearing'* I obtained from a Shaman named Lauren some weeks earlier had kick-started something in my subconscious. I wasn't dismissing anything as a root cause, but I decided it was time to get out the laptop and start typing.

The more I typed, the more that came out. Some days, it was all I could do to keep up. Other days I sat at the beach and thought about the past, about memory; about what time travel could look like. I began to revisit an old topic for me – that of reincarnation.

Coming from a Judeo-Christian background, I was taught to believe in the notion of incarnation; a one-time trip down from the ether to earth. Seventy years to get it right and then the judgment. Back to heaven if you make a passing grade[78] but otherwise eternal damnation.

I left that idea some time back and have wandered – mostly without resolution - around both Eastern and Western philosophy. I don't have any solid answers anymore, but more to the point, I am not constrained by unanswered questions.

---

[78]   The FAA universally considers a passing grade as 70% or better. Can we get this standard applied, or is it 100% or nothing? Grace might suggest that 51% is a more equitable benchmark.

If I had a strong belief in reincarnation[79], it might help rationalize my deep and abiding attachment to Rose, Jack and the movie *Titanic*.

Forever, movies that portray a deep spiritual connection beyond death have held sway: *Always, What Dreams May Come, Ghost, Cloud Atlas* and others. Then there's the monster awakening movie *The Matrix*, which hit me light a bolt of enlightened awareness.

Family Man with Nicholas Cage was another movie in which the character is shifted overnight into a completely different reality, a completely different but parallel story.

At the end of *Titanic* as the camera switches back to present day, the recovery crew and Rose are reviewing dive film and talking.

"We never found anything on Jack," said one dive team member to the 100-year-old Rose. "There was no record at all."

"No, there wouldn't be, would there?" she reflected.

> *"And I've never spoken of him until now; not to anyone - not even your grandfather. A woman's heart is a deep ocean of secrets. But now you know there was a man named Jack Dawson - and that he saved me in every way that a person can be saved. I don't even have a picture of him.*
>
> *He exists now only in my memory."*

Bill Mahoney exists now only in my memory, deeply flawed and subject to mental revisions as I think about the story now and again.

---

[79]   I once paid for a hypnotic regression session to explore potential past lives. I was put in a deeply relaxed state of meditation and challenged to float up in the ether, hang around for a while and slowly return to earth. When the hypnotherapist asked me to look down at my feet and describe what I saw, I had to say, "regrettably, I still see my Wingtips." I got my money back.

For the longest time I thought the most logical and only way to view my life was on a linear timeline. We're born, we have a childhood, we are teens, we move through our 20s, 30s, 40s, 50s, 60s - and if bloodlines and fate are kind, into the stratosphere of later life where action and deeds are supplanted almost entirely by memory.

Lately I have come to think that the idea of a linear timeline is just a tool we have invented to help make sense of things. This happened, then that happened, then another thing happened and now here we are.

Albert Einstein is widely misquoted as having said that "time is what keeps everything from happening at once." The actual author is probably Ray Cummings, and first appeared in his 1919 short story 'The Girl in the Golden Atom.'

Perhaps time is just an artificial construct to help us think about things. Maybe linear timelines are more akin to a coffee mug's handle; something convenient to grab on to.

It appears we live largely - and perhaps for the most part subconsciously - in our stories. It can be a house of mirrors in which one image dominates all others and seems to cloud and determine our paths forward.

Those internal stories shout at us loudly, coloring, informing and limiting our view.

We have a traumatic childhood, and that story takes on a life of its own. We go through a divorce or three and that story colors every other relationship. I keep coming back to Anais Nin who said that *we don't see the world as it is, we see it as we are.*

We spend a lifetime accumulating stories that both originate and live largely in our private head space. Some stories have more emotional attachment than others, but in the end, we seem to line these stories up in chronological order.

What we need - what I need - is a way to detach myself from linear thinking.

Maybe I should think about my stories like stones scattered in a huge field. Some stones are round and bland, not worth much of a second glance. Some stones are sharp and jagged and need to be handled with care. Finally, some

177

stones are like diamonds, multi-faceted and endlessly mesmerizing. These are the ones worth deep contemplation.

We pick up this story and examine it like a diamond, turning it this way and that, observing how the light interplays with every facet. The trick with these diamonds is to observe and contemplate the story without being controlled by it.

For most of us, these diamonds have subconsciously controlled us. These stories, whatever they are, become the defining pillars of our life. They turn into constraints that limit our freedom of movement and tie us deeply to the past. Finally, we place these diamonds in a row and say, *'that's my life.'*

Maybe it would serve me better if I let go of the notion that all the stones need to be placed in some kind of linear fashion.

Perhaps the sorting for all of us should go something like this: *'the green ones go over here, the reds ones in another pile, the hateful ones in their own corner.'* Then we could begin to see patterns, habits and conditioning that has constricted our vision, clouded our sovereignty and kept us walking in the dark.

In this manner - when we are done navel gazing - we can just walk away from the field and say, *"well that was interesting, but what's in store for me today?"*

We detach our emotions from these intense and formative stories. We let go of judgment, self-condemnation, fear, anger and whatever else has controlled and limited us.

We learn to walk with our stories, to examine them from time to time but not to be controlled by them.

Perhaps this is time travel; a sort of wandering and dreaming that lets us move in and out of time as we desire.

I am Bill Mahoney

I am eternal.

I am just one story among millions.

Bill Mahoney

Made in the USA
Columbia, SC
18 November 2024

46750486R00104